PRAISE FOR L

"I really enjoyed reading this book. It inspired me. The author's ability to capture the magic of what the natural world shares with us is breathtaking. I also think she has presented a powerful set of tools and achievable guidelines for all peoples to follow. Hunter has also masterfully shared some of life's sacred teachings that nature gifts us: gratitude, humility, passion, love, presence, honesty, integrity, and a few more that are not close to my tongue right now."

— TERRY KEM, CyberTracker certified;
founder of Deerdance Tracking School

"This book is a unique combination of inspiration for nature connection, practical guide to outdoor safety and comfort, tracking and trailing guidebook, love letter to bears and cougars, and storybook of a wild life lived well. The author continues to break stereotypes about who belongs outdoors, and beautifully shows that we all can reach for a bit of wildness outside ourselves.

" If you aren't sure about the idea of spending a day in nature by yourself, Linda is the person to talk you through everything from how to go to the bathroom, how to make clear decisions, how tracks can guide you to animals, what to do if you meet a bear, and how to be safe as a solo woman hiker or biker. Her stories reflect a lifetime of exciting, practical, humorous, and humble lessons about living with wildness."

–KIMBER NELSON, CyberTracker certified,
Cascadia Wild Wolverine Tracking Project

"Someone brand new to the woods will find this an excellent primer, while more experienced folks will still very much enjoy identifying with Linda's journey and finding practical tips. The writing is lovely. The book is well-organized and has a logical flow, with an excellent mix of what it means to connect deeply with nature as a spiritual being combined with practical tips like what to put in your backpack."

—DAVID BARBUR, author of the *Tye Caine Wilderness Mysteries*

"As a nature lover since childhood days, the message of *Lonesome for Wilderness* deeply resonated with me. A call to action when the hectic world threatens to overwhelm you ... to find your way into the wilds. And the author supplies you with the tools and ways to build your confidence to do so. Well written, and easy to digest as the author shares her knowledge and experience through the art of storytelling. Highly recommended."

—INDY QUILLEN, author of the *Fox Walker Novels*

"How does one learn to be a tracker? If you are a woman, how can you stay safe in the wilderness while also enjoying all it has to offer? Don't believe the naysayers. Yes, you can have safe adventures and experience the amazing world of animal tracking.

"This book provides excellent advice from one of the top trackers in the world. Using Linda's techniques, you will soon be experiencing the joy of tracking animals that you may have previously feared. Knowledge is power. Once you understand these animals, you will learn to respect them and to be around them safely. The author learned about bears and understands them enough to be safely in their presence. She knows what to watch for and how an animal might behave in an encounter with a human. You can learn this skill too, and have your own amazing adventures in the outdoors!...I loved the book. It was fantastic!"

—KIM A. CABRERA, Beartracker Nature Films;
CyberTracker Track & Sign Specialist

"...I just read the chapter on trailing. I appreciate how the author has it spread around her experience, and balanced as an art. Not just following animals, not just following people. [She tells her] experience of following the stories and I like that. She includes pointers for learning without being a 'how to' book. I especially appreciate the last sentence of the chapter; deer do make our lives more interesting. I can't point to a better teacher for learning to track."

—BRIAN McCONNELL, Trailing Specialist, CyberTracker North America

"A wonderful guide to help nature lovers engage with the lives of birds and insects in backyards and parks, or bears and lions deep in the wild. Full of great tips and stories on the rewards of becoming a nature sleuth, quietly observant, tracking and interpreting scent marks, feeding signs, nest sites, and following trails that can lead to unforgettable encounters with wildlife."

—JUDY MALONE, founder of Protect Our Bears Ontario

LONESOME FOR WILDERNESS

Linda,
Keep being Wild!

Linda J. Hunter

ALSO BY LINDA JO HUNTER

Lonesome for Bears

A Woman's Journey in the Tracks of the Wilderness

Lonesome for Wilderness

Tracking and Trailing in Forest, Desert, or Your Own Back Yard

Linda Jo Hunter

Jolibro Publishing
La Mesa, California

Jolibro Publishing
www.jolibro.com

Library of Congress Control Number: 2024932421

ISBN 978-1-953474-10-0 (paperback)
ISBN 978-1-953474-11-7 (ebook)

First Edition

To my crabs, my Cancer-born best friends:
Mike McHugh you are simply the best in every way.
Jane Doudney you are my most valuable friend.

Contents

"To the attentive eye, each moment of the year has its own beauty, and in the same field, it beholds, every hour, a picture which was never seen before, and which shall never be seen again."

—Ralph Waldo Emerson

~1~

Your Wild Streak

When we recognize our wild streak and our animalness, the world makes much more sense. Like when you're in a meeting, school, or church and you find yourself looking at the clouds out the window—that's your wild streak. If you are talking with someone outside and you are aware of the breeze on your cheek, the song a bird sings, or crickets and frogs, that's your wild streak. Every time you notice a beautiful sunset, the soothing sound of rain, and the beauty of big snowflakes drifting down, you are tuning into your wild streak.

Some people have more wild than others, and some of us develop a healthy streak of wild during our lifetimes. It's not such a long way from being happy to see fledgling birds begging for food—to lightly putting your fingers in a mountain lion track and feeling the wonder and power of an animal you used to fear.

One day you may see a spider in your house and freak the heck out, thinking of the spider biting you or creeping around your face while you sleep. Then, if you watch the spider for a while, you might wonder what its life is like. Instead of grabbing a shoe to squash it, you might notice the elaborate way the spider has installed itself in your house, on guard to kill and eat enemies who are way more dangerous than grizzly bears; those little tiny viruses and mold motes that can kill us. You might decide then that spiders can be good roommates. Perhaps you'll become a person who lies down in a grassy bear bed near a ridge top, just to see what the bear could see from there.

Getting more in touch with the wild can give a person basic happiness, joy, safety, and sanity. It's really an easy corner to turn once you get started.

"Go outside," our mother said, and maybe yours did too. Your teachers send you out to recess and you find yourself outdoors at different times of your life. What no one tells us, as we meander our way through a human life, is that being outside is where you will find yourself.

My friend Jane was sitting on a log with her head down. We'd ridden our bikes back into the forest where there were no cars. I wondered if there was something wrong with her as I tried to find huckleberries up the hill from where she sat. Finally, a good twenty minutes later, I came down to ask what she was doing.

She was watching ants.

Ants can be fascinating. They have organized lives that vary depending on their species. Some ants move house, all at once, creating what looks like a fat snake track on the land. Others walk down trails carrying a moth wing in the breeze, defying the laws of gravity and strength.

Jane and I talked about ants. We realized that if we could speak with them, they wouldn't know much about our world. They don't even know about New York City or airplanes and the internet. We know just about as much about their world. Who knows, maybe they know all about reincarnation and astral existence, mind reading and mystic arts. They may feel sorry for us poor humans.

If you feel your wild streak pulling at you, this book is for you. No matter how wild you are now, you can get more wild. My way for you to do that is to do it comfortably, at your pace, with the ability to let it take you where you need to go.

The things that hold you to a life of going from car to house, and store to work, on cement walkways and freeways, are things you can work around. All you need is the desire to grow that wild part of you. The hesitancy to leave the comfort of our dwellings and shelters and go talk to ants has to do with just not knowing what it is that we don't know. We are all beginners, myself included.

No matter what we think we know, there is always more. Always.

~2~

Roughing it

There is no good reason for a person to be uncomfortable outdoors. Just no reason at all. Except, of course, poor planning. Or letting someone else plan and control your adventures.

"Roughing it" is a term that sticks to hiking, camping, and venturing outdoors. If you think about it, there's a macho culture around wilderness that makes it seem romantic and adventurous to harden up, power through, do without, and suffer.

The White man and the conquering of the "Wild West" gave us masses of literature and story that evoked this concept of conquering heroes and hardship. Zane Gray, Louis L'Amour, Jack London, and many other writers of the Western genre all seemed to follow the same code: White men are heroes with incredible integrity and the ability to endure. Women, Native Americans, Mexicans, and immigrants from anywhere but Europe are to be rescued, held hostage, murdered, or jilted as the White man rides off into the sunset.

This generalization, as it occurs in literature and movies, may be entertaining but ultimately it makes getting outside fraught with fears for most of us. And for White men, there is the expectation that they can conquer anything. All of which is something we all need to get over.

One of the reasons *The Journals of [Merriweather] Lewis and [William] Clark* are so interesting is that they are not fiction. However, they are the version written by the White men on the expedition. Getting a glimpse of what we really want to know can only be done by reading between the lines.

Sacagawea, for instance, was a Native American woman who accompanied Lewis and Clark to the West Coast in one of the most celebrated explorations of the United States. In digging into her story, I found several incidents in the journals of the trip where she used her common sense and the upbringing of her culture to save lives. Although she was treated about the same as Seaman, the expedition's Newfoundland dog, she saved the men from scurvy by collecting wild greens. As the hardships multiplied, she was able to take care of herself. Her role in the journey has been romanticized in modern literature, but if you know much about the lives of indigenous women in the early 1800s and read the journals themselves, you find that she was won in a poker game at age sixteen and was taken on the trip as a wife/slave/servant to a French-Canadian trapper and trader, Toussaint Charbonneau.

It's true that by the time they reached the big ocean near Astoria, Oregon, she had earned enough respect to be asked her opinion by the leaders. Many of the men must have watched her take care of herself and her baby and learned a few things. It's not a stretch of my imagination that her way of being comfortable on the land must have kept her alive. Unlike the White men she was with, who had unrealistic expectations placed on them from leaders (like that they would obey orders, and that they were to be tough and keep up, no matter what), Sacagawea knew how to move and survive with the land.

Today it's, "Honey, let's go camping, we can take the kids, it'll be fun."

In that sentence are born two different realities. His is a picture of him conquering the wild with his trusty axe and a beer in one hand. Hers is wildflowers, peaceful reading under a tree while the kids play quietly on the bank of a gentle stream.

For singles, it's the person you've been seeing who says, "Hey, I know this place we can go camp in the mountains and there are some great hikes nearby. Come on…what do you say? I'll take care of everything…you just need to bring yourself, oh, and maybe a jacket."

The first clue that you should run away is the "I'll take care of everything."

Why? Because for many the idea of a weekend spent camping and hiking does not include knowing what weather changes to expect, keeping food at safe temperatures, creating an insect-free bed, or finding privacy. They may not even know how to read a map. Your companion may think the GPS in their phone is all they need.

Then there's the idea that a shot of whiskey will make up for freezing feet and poison oak.

There are quite a few so-called "outdoor" traditions. The stereotypes are strong. Like a smoky fire and gooey s'mores. Eating hot dogs, which you never eat at home, isn't going to make you feel any better.

Instead, think about how you can stay overnight in the wild and make little impact, and how you can stay comfortable and safe without chopping wood, hauling stones, or rubbing sticks together to light the fire. The gear exists to make an overnight stay clean and simple with good food and sound sleep.

Some people can't feature coming home without smelling like smoke and having to clean up wet sticky gear. An efficient propane stove that leaves very little imprint on the land might leave them unsatisfied. It's true that people can get away with roughing it and have a great time, but it's not the only way.

The best possible companion for wilderness work is someone who is smart and able—and who thinks it's a good idea to be comfortable.

Once you learn to be self-sufficient—a solo worker or traveler who has the basics covered—you'll want to be with other people who are on that same level.

One warm August night I was with a team of two other search-and-rescue volunteers at two in the morning. We had hit a cliff, and going down it without rope gear in the dark wasn't a wise thing. Our team leader decided to head back to base instead of being macho by making our way down anyway. But not right away, as we would just get another assignment and we were all three tired, hungry, scratched up, and frustrated. Instead, we found a place to sit, made hot drinks, and took the snacks out of our packs. We treated ourselves to a quiet rest away from the chaos of base camp and the frenzy to find the lost subject.

While we sat, enjoying the soft night air, we talked quietly about the lost person and where he could be. The huckleberries were thick on the cliff edge and we could smell their sweet, pungent aroma coming up from the valley. We all thought it was possible that the older man who was lost had been lured that way by berries and found he couldn't climb back up. I believe our team leader shared our thinking on where the man might be to the deputies running the search.

When we got back to camp sure enough, we had another assignment, but we were ready for it. Having a team leader who understood what we needed was the key to a successful night.

The subject, by the way, was located alive and well the next morning, a mile or so down the cliff on which we rested.

~ 3 ~
Going Alone

I remember one New Year's Eve when my husband, who was a banquet manager at a resort, wouldn't be home until the wee hours of the night. I decided to go snowshoeing and have dinner under the stars.

I packed up my car with my snow clothes, snowshoes, and pack. I brought my little propane stove, which fits in my stainless cooking cup, and a nice soup to heat up to go with my sandwich. I planned hot chocolate for dessert. I picked a spot at an elevation where I knew the snow wouldn't be too deep so I wouldn't have to break trail. I carried three kinds of flashlights and extra batteries with me, even though the moon was due to come up at seven-thirty that night. I took a pad to sit on and stuck my bear-sized pepper spray in the front holder on my backpack.

As expected, I saw no one on the road to Rush Creek. There were no cars parked at the snow parks. I found no fresh tracks, except for elk, on the closed road I chose to walk up. Every human I knew was at a party somewhere and at least thirty miles from where I was.

The moonrise was golden through the fir trees and the silence of the trail was broken by the soft swish sound my snowshoes made. When I got high enough up the road to be able to see the surrounding hills, I made my "quiet sit" spot. I mounded up a table out of snow and made a comfortable sitting spot in a snowbank with my insulated pad in the bottom. I heated up my soup and ate to the accompaniment of some late juncos who were flitting around the edge of the trees and making their little twittering sounds.

As I sat back with my hot chocolate to take in the moment with all my senses, I realized how incredibly blessed I was to feel so comfortable and at home in this special place. I could hear everything, I knew right where I was, and the clear air enhanced the sparkle of the snow in moonlight and the delicate etching of ice on the trees. The feelings of peace, well-being, and joy of life were my New Year's gifts to myself.

But then I heard what sounded like an ambulance siren. Somewhere behind me on the ridge, a piercing howl was joined by other voices. The noise bounced off the hills and seemed to ring non-existent bells in the tree limbs. The yips of joy following the initial song clued me in to a coyote pack.

A big smile spread across my face and I turned to see if they were visible on the ridge. There was nothing I could see. A few minutes of silence passed before another pack, on the ridge in front of me, added their unique voices to the night. Staying still and comfortable, I listened for quite a while as they maneuvered around the hills doing coyote things. I'm sure they knew I was there.

It was a very memorable night, attending a coyote's New Year instead of a human one. It was such a great experience that I wrote about it for a local outdoors magazine.

A month or two later, I was at work in the county assessor's office when a guy came in who wanted some map help. He asked me for a map of the Rush Creek area. As I rustled through the pages in the map book looking for the right section, I asked him if he had ever been there before.

He held up a magazine and said he hadn't but that he'd read this great story about a guy who snowshoed there at night, alone.

I looked at him over the top of my readers and asked, "What makes you think it was a guy?"

"Well," he said, "it was at night and I just figured..." He stopped when he saw my expression.

"Look at the byline," I said.

"Linda Hunter," he read slowly.

I smiled and said, "Yes, that was me."

His face went white. It was a few seconds before he could speak. He looked at the story again, then back at me, trying to fit my image into his preconceived notion of a solo nocturnal wilderness traveler.

By time I gave him his map copy he was very apologetic. He said he could hardly believe that a guy would be out there alone at night. He thought it was a very cool thing to do, but it never occurred to him that women can do that too.

I gave him the map copy and wished him a good time.

~ Making Your Own Tracks ~

I'm betting you've been told in words, gestures, and insinuations that you can't possibly be thinking about going out in the wilderness alone.

"Never go alone," "Hike in groups," and "Make a lot of noise" are all things that keep agencies from worrying about the liability of neophyte recreational hordes using public lands. It's also the way your family, friends, and acquaintances disrespect your ability to take care of yourself. I know that's harsh, that they caution you out of love and caring for you, but no one tells me that anymore. Instead, they ask if they can go with me.

Here's the deal, though. I don't take people with me unless I am getting paid. Because, if they can't go alone, that means they need me to guide them. Guiding is a professional endeavor. (We'll address that later.) I do, however, go with people who can take care of themselves. That's just plain fun.

Think of all the dangerous things you already do alone. Like going to a gas station, shopping for food, or just walking down a city street. Personally, I feel much safer in a wild landscape than any human-constructed habitat.

The wilderness might even be safer when you're solo. When you're alone, you only have one person's energy to deal with. The attention you give to keeping up with someone else, keeping a conversation going, and meeting their expectations for the day, doesn't seem like much until you experience a day without those subtle pressures. When there are no distractions, your attention can be completely directed to what is around you and what is going on. Because you are paying complete attention to your surroundings, you will have a pretty good assessment of what other beings are in your area. You'll smell the smoke of a campfire, the sudden quietness of the birds, the distant hum of an ATV, or the rumble of a truck. You'll be able to hear the crunch of gravel, the splash of puddles, or the sound of breaking sticks. You won't walk past a danger sign. There's a reason it's against the law to drive and be on your phone. It's been proven that talking to someone else diverts your awareness and causes you to be late in making judgements about safety.

You also take better care of yourself when you're alone. You'll think twice before jumping into a creek with the intention of landing on the rock in the middle. You won't put off having to pee or take off your shoe to deal with a hot spot. You'll be more likely to put on your jacket when you need it, or stop to drink water. You'll eat when you're hungry and rest when you're tired.

If you are walking down a trail without distractions (a dog can also be a distraction), you will hear everything. It helps if you are a little afraid. That makes you pay attention and not wander off somewhere in a daydream. The staccato chirps of a bird alarming or the shrill alarms of squirrels will make an impression on you. You'll be looking at things in a new way. Your mind will sort out the movement of plants due to breeze from the flash of a furry body. The scent of flowers may change as you walk to the scent of a dead animal. Even the activity of bugs means something, which you might definitely miss if someone you are walking with is talking to you.

It wouldn't take too long for you to get comfortable with short solo hikes. Then, when you hear people coming down the trail and you step off into a shaded spot and stand still, you can see them walk right by without noticing you, as they are completely absorbed in what they are talking about. The only person who may see you is the straggler walking behind the group, or definitely the off-leash dog.

The skills needed to keep yourself safe can be practiced and improved. Spending time alone in wild places improves your eyesight, your senses of smell and hearing. You become more aware of how your hair moves in the slightest breeze and the dryness or humidity in the air.

When you learn solo comfort and peace, the animals notice. On a bike ride by myself in a remote spot, a shaded glade by a bubbling spring called to me. The sun was warm and I had a few hours to spend. I decided to use part of my time just sitting there, quietly. It was spring and the snows had just retreated. Animals were out looking for food, love, and nest-building materials. Teenage animals were learning about life and their place in the world.

A young Douglas squirrel was trying out different trees overhead, but being quiet about it. When it noticed me, sitting like any other bump on a log, it gave a burst of shocked chatter. Then, it was quiet. Before long, I heard tiny toenails scrabbling on the bark of the tree just behind me. I looked just in time to see the squirrel duck.

Within a half hour, it was on the ground circling me, seemingly wondering if I were alive. I averted my eyes so I wouldn't force a confrontation.

The little animal was so brave that he finally came up and shot out a paw to touch me. I gave no reaction and he did it a second time. There was no way I could hold my laughter after that, so he retreated to a nearby branch to scold me.

A precious moment that wouldn't have happened if I hadn't been alone.

A wild traveler will miss the essence of nature if they don't go solo sometimes—the utter peace and rejuvenation that can happen when you meet the wild alone.

I'm not the only solo adventurer. I asked Kim Cabrera about it. She is a tracker who has a big influence on people who track, via her online educational posts. Kim has been a tracker for more than forty-five years and I've known her, or of her, for almost as long. She was instrumental in the early days of ISPT (International Society of Professional Trackers), taking over, with Del Morris, the maintenance of its online presence when I quit putting out the newsletter. We held several conferences of ISPT and Kim was instrumental in all of them. I've enjoyed some great tracking days with Kim, and I hope to have many more.

Kim told me, "I always go alone. It's very rare for me to go anywhere outdoors with other people. Mostly that happens when I'm teaching a class or leading a walk. Otherwise, it's just me."

She says she stays safe by staying away from other people. She's been known to step off a trail and conceal herself within brush or behind trees to let people pass without her being seen. Because there are a lot of illegal marijuana crops in her area in the woods, she's pretty careful.

"When I am outdoors, I never bring distractions with me. I don't own a smart phone, I don't listen to music and don't use earphones. I want to hear just the sounds of nature. That's important to me. I rarely listen to music unless I am driving."

"But..." I can hear you say. "But what about getting lost or killed or having to be rescued?"

Yes, there is that. If you read this whole book, practice and learn, you will be able to make yourself safe. I can't do it for you. No one can. But you can do it for yourself, and personally, I think you deserve it.

~4~

Enhancing Your Wild Streak

Having watched people over the years turn their adventures into the deeper experience of natural observation, I know a few things you can do to get much more meaning out of your bike rides, kayak trips, and hikes. Books and classes only go so far. Pretty soon you'll want to take the next step.

You can start with your own property if you live with wild animals. Or if not, pick a place, preferably in a national park or somewhere that is not a popular tourist destination, and find a little corner that you feel safe in. Feeling safe there should be the result of you checking out the spot, knowing how to get in and out several ways, and looking to see if there are other human tracks. Pick a place to sit where you can see well and have something behind you to block passage, or that you can hear if something comes from behind. For instance, don't sit by a noisy stream where you can't hear or in a spot where you can't see around you.

Once you've found a spot that speaks to you, visit it frequently. It would be good if you can sit there, quietly, for a couple of hours. During this time, the animals will forget you're there. I find that they relax when the human has been still and quiet for about twenty minutes.

I often sit with a notebook and pencil to jot down notes or sketch. But, it is pretty important that you not spend time on your phone or get lost in writing. You're there to observe as much as you can about what is going on around you.

It's amazing how much you can learn from this exercise. You can tell which birds live there and which ones are passing through. You can observe which squirrels live in which trees and how they protect their territories. You might see an animal you didn't even know lived there.

In your notebook, do a bird's eye view map of your spot and put in the spots where various animals eat, sleep, make beds and nests, and where they overlap with other animals. Write down their interactions with each other, and with you. Even the bugs in the area have patterns and things to teach. Every habitat is different and constantly changing. Your records of how the animals use the habitat will lead to fascinating wisdom that deepens over the years.

After thirty-plus years of tracking, I have a whole lot of spots where I spend time quietly sitting and observing. In each of them, if I haven't visited for a while, I can immediately see things that have changed, like a limb missing off a tree, or a patch of new plants.

Jon Young, who wrote *Animal Tracking Basics,* calls this a "quiet sit spot." Hopefully you can find his book, as it details ways of doing this very well. He also wrote *What the Robin Knows,* which should be on your reading list because bird language is something every tracker must know about, listen to, and never ignore.

Birds are definitely busy little bodies. They talk a lot about everything that is going on. If you can discern which calls are the ones they use for alarm, and which ones they use between them to locate and gossip, then you can use them for your lookout. Birds see everything, and they make different noises depending on what's going on from their point of view.

At your quiet spot, you can learn which birds hang around or nest there and what they are likely to be upset about. Then, when the day comes that they make some sort of noise you haven't heard before, you'll know there's a difference.

Squirrels also make alarm calls. They are probably the most vocal animals of all. You might be used to them announcing you to every animal for miles around any time you go for a hike. There is a point in your self-education in "wild walking" that they'll stop doing this. It will happen after your movements change and your intentions and energy become clear to them. Then whenever you hear them, you'll know it wasn't you who caused the ruckus.

After you have established a quiet spot, learned a small area in detail, and become comfortable and safe spending time there, it's time to take your knowledge on the road.

Hiking, snowshoeing, bicycling, and kayaking can all get you to special places where animals live. If you are lucky enough to own a horse, the natural world is easy to find.

What you don't want to make a habit is going by motor, whether it is a four-wheeler or snowmobile, or anything noisier than a car. The time it takes for animals to go back to what they were doing after that kind of interruption can be long—if you haven't moved them completely out of the area.

There are, of course, exceptions. Sometimes the only access to a wild area involves some kind of motor. The noise factor is one of the reasons I like to use my electric bike, as it's quiet and can be ridden at a slow, non-disturbing pace.

And don't forget about visual tracking. As you become more aware of your surroundings, you are going to want to learn to see where animals have walked, slept, and eaten.

As you learn to take care of yourself and go more often to wild places, you'll start to notice the tracks and signs that animals leave. Learning to read this visual language is a key to learning of what animals do and why, and your personal place in the world.

In 2011, I was helping scout for an area to hold an evaluation for CyberTracker North America, which is an organization for tracker education. It was my home turf so I had a couple of areas in mind when I started out.

One of the spots was private land with a small access road. When we turned off the main road into this area, I saw a couple of ravens sitting in a tree. When we shut off the car and got out, we quickly noticed that there were about fifty ravens. They all seemed to be concentrating their attention on one area. We'd been told not to go tracking in the areas they might use for the evaluation but this was just too tempting. We had to see what was going on. What we found was a recently killed elk in a dry stream bed.

It was pretty obvious that the main predators were still around. We backed out of the area gently, so as not to disturb the site.

Of course the evaluation staff wanted to use that spot. It turned out to be an incredible day spent examining all the evidence left behind by all the animals who benefited from the kill. I think I learned more that day than I had in the previous ten years of tracking. I can still picture every detail, from raven pellets to cougar scent-marking scrapes.

Although tracking and traveling alone are good ways to learn, you may also reach a point where you wish for another mind or two to bounce ideas off. Several times over the years I have enjoyed the luxury of a tracking companion who is as crazy interested in the whole thing as I am.

My current tracking buddy, Jane Doudney, and I have developed good nonverbal communication. She finds something and goes completely still. I can read this body language out of the corner of my eye. If it's really good, I will get a one-word pronouncement like, "Huh!" Or maybe, "Cool!" if it's really, really good.

Then we examine the sign, the area around it, the trees, the road if there is one, and look for trails. We listen to the birds, squirrels, and insects for extra activity and start to put together the story.

It was a Fall day when we paused on our bikes at a spot we

visit often. It's a narrow gravel road that passes between a rock cliff and a small river. Animals and humans use this narrow passage to get from one area to another. It sort of went like this:

"Jane, is that a bear track?"

"Sure looks like it to me."

"But how did a bear get there?" The track was in the middle of the cliff face on some of the trapped dirt.

"Hum."

We looked for tracks coming in and out of the spot. We walked around slowly, looking at the thing from different angles. At first, the bear track looked completely isolated, as there weren't any tracks from the bottom going up to it and the bear was clearly headed uphill. Then I noticed an indistinct disturbed area next to, but below the track.

"Wow," I said, "I think the bear fell and landed just below the track."

"Fell there?"

"Yeah, look at that loose dirt and overturned rock. I think that big divot might be where a butt landed."

"Oh. I see it. Yeah, look—you can see some telltale sign higher up. There's a flower pushed down, along with some leaves."

"Yup, I see that too. But what in the heck makes a bear fall off a cliff? And then it looks like he took off uphill. Look just above that track; you can see where his nails dug in for purchase."

"Oh wow. Yeah, just above that is a spot it jumped to. Look there! You can see divots for all four paws!"

We scoured that area for more clues. We found vehicle tracks that were also fresh, and to the side of the cliff area, we found two spots where humans had scrambled up the slope, heading for the top of the cliff.

Suspicion made us reexamine the tracks again. Jane saw it first. Just where the flower was pushed down, she noticed a fresh crease in a tree where a bullet had hit it. It was right above where the bear had been feeding on flowers. Then the bear must have fallen and left the quick-exit trail we could see from the ground.

Putting more clues together by using our binoculars, for instance to determine the angle of the bullet mark, we deduced between the two of us that:

(a) A vehicle had come around the corner,
(b) the occupants saw a bear on the face of the rockslide,
(c) they shot at it,
(d) the bear fell down part way,
(e) then it took off straight up the slope, and
(f) the humans got out of the vehicle and tried to chase after it by heading up just past the slide.

Because it was not open hunting season, we reported it. The Fish and Game officer followed the tracks of the two humans up the hill but determined the bear got away.

This happened in a spot we monitor often. Because we ride by there a couple of times a month all summer, anything unusual sticks out and we are able to discern new animal sign from old.

Some animals visit the same place as often as we do. We've noticed that a bobcat leaves scent-mark scrapes, tracks, and scats on a regular basis. Sometimes a coyote thinks it will cover up the bobcat sign with its own scat. Just recently a cougar left its scat right next to the bobcat. If we could smell things more completely, perhaps the subtleties of the olfactory messages would surprise us. It's still educational to know that these "social media" posts left by multiple species exist.

Before we leave the idea of the quiet sit, or becoming your own trail camera, I need to throw in a caution. You can get too comfortable.

One day I was driving along on my way to join friends for a bike ride when I saw some ravens fly up from beside the road. I stopped, backed up, and got out to see what they were doing. A smallish dead deer lay just off the road. I quickly memorized the spot and determined that I would come back at the end of the day to check it out; I was late for meeting my friends.

At the end of the day, I spotted the tree I had memorized and stopped to look more closely at the deer. It was gone.

But as I slowly walked the road, I could see smashed down vegetation where the deer had been dragged up out of the ditch and into the forest. When I got on top of the berm next to the drag marks, I found cougar tracks alongside the path of the dead animal. I was able to follow the trail into the trees. At the end of the trail I spotted what was left of the deer. I rough-estimated that about fifteen pounds of the animal were missing. There were some tasty bits left, though, and I could tell by the fresh tracks that the eater was still there, probably waiting for me to leave. I thought it would be a wonderful opportunity for me to see the cougar come back.

I went back to the road and walked about fifty feet down to where a side road cut back up to the woods. I walked up there quietly and found a spot where I could see the remains. I got my camera ready and settled into some deep vegetation to watch. I got so comfortably settled that I fell asleep.

I'm not sure what woke me, but I immediately had a talk with myself about being too comfortable in the woods. I didn't get to see the cougar because I made myself go home. Jeez.

~ 5 ~

Building Skills

The first animal I learned to track was a teenager. I could tell whenever I came home if he had brought friends over. There would be details left behind: candy wrappers in the trash can, moved couch cushions, leaves on the carpet, and debris wherever they went. I could even tell where else they had gone by the quality of the muddy shoe prints on the deck.

Tracking all the other animals, although it involves paw prints and their recognition, is a reading of the entire habitat. Learning about it is a different journey for each tracker, although we all end up at the same place. That place is an ever-enlarging appetite for learning more about the natural world and the animals that live there.

There are excellent tracking teachers and classes around the world. A good way to start is to sign up for a class nearby, buy some field guides, and start the journey. It's important, though, to realize that you're going to need more than one teacher, and one of them is you.

I started with books on tracking, compelled by a surprise and scary encounter with a black bear. Of course if I were to have that same encounter now, I would be moved to laughter instead of knocking knees and panic breathing. My tracking journey has taken me to places where I've literally lived with both black and grizzly bears.

Field guides about tracking are important. Learning the foot morphology of different species is the best way to start, even if it doesn't "take" right away. I distinctly remember reading about the number of toes a raccoon has, then squirrels, voles, moles, frogs, and weasels. Then saying to myself, " I will never remember all this!" And, I didn't remember it.

I made little cheat sheets, and even wrote a poem about digit numbers, but the missing ingredient in all those things is the real-life track, which never looks like the drawings in field guides.

One bike ride I took by myself brought me to some cool-looking tracks in the dust on the road where I stopped at the top of a grade to rest. I studied them, noticing the long toes attached like cigars to a palm pad. I ran down the list of mid-sized tracks: bobcat, cougar, coyote...and then finally remembered to count the toes. Five toes! That eliminated most of the animals I already knew about. What I didn't notice, until I looked the tracks up again, was that the front and hind track lay side by side. When I found the tracks in my field guide, I noticed that it mentioned that a common raccoon gait was this unique placing. Because I had seen it in the dirt, the raccoon tracks became alive for me.

You'd think that after learning what raccoon tracks looked like, I would always be able to recognize them. However, in order to be able to quickly recognize tracks of an animal, you need to see those tracks hundreds of times in different substrates and conditions; in dust and deep mud, on the cement driveway, in the grass, on the trash can, in the bottom of a puddle underwater, in rocks…you get the idea. Then, when you do see a track, you need to be conscious of noticing how many digits there are, what the spacing of those digits is, if there are claw marks or not, the arrangement of the toes around the inter-digital pad (palm pad), and a dozen other little details that are called the morphology of the paw.

I spent a few years just looking for tracks. I stopped at every mud puddle, searched out sandy areas and stream banks. When I found tracks, I wasn't always able to identify them, and sometimes I got it wrong. The field guides definitely help but things happen in the wild in imperfect ways. Deer step on their own hoof prints in a way that makes it look like a big animal with four digits. It seems like we all get fooled by that one at least once. Elk slip in the mud and make a slide that looks like an otter playing. Beavers drag trees to the water, making huge trails that can be a real puzzle as they wipe out their own tracks. The snow can make a vole trail look like Godzilla walked there, and the toes which normally ride up the leg of some animals and never register may suddenly show up in soft substrate.

Incorporating the associated sign with tracks helps. For instance, learning what the animal eats and what feeding signs are present with the tracks, or what scent-marking behavior might be in the vicinity. All animal behavior registers on the land. They leave scent marks, feeding sign, and resting beds, or evidence of nest gathering, dust baths, and rutting wallows. You might find nests, feathers, bones, skulls, snagged fur, dens, and scat. Sometimes they leave really unique sign that is fun to figure out.

Last summer, Jane and I found a brown and gold Forest

Service sign on a back road that had been bitten up by bears. The bear (or bears) who marked it left muddy paw prints as well, so it was pretty easy to see who had done it.

When we looked at the back of the sign, though, we found a muddy body print where a very messy bear had rubbed on the sign, leaving swirls of fur marks outlining its body. Very interesting to find, with the actual hairs attached in some spots. We found it almost as entertaining as seeing the bear.

It's not possible to become a tracker who never makes a mistake. Animals do whatever the heck they want and sometimes we just can't figure it out. Quite a few of the mistakes I've made over the years have involved big dog tracks.

Not long ago, on a back road in the snow, I was all excited to find some huge canine tracks maintaining the wild dog style of a straight-ahead, no-nonsense gait. My wolf wishful thinking got ahead of me. An inside voice said it couldn't be and another one said, why not?

I kept investigating in the area, trying to find scat or more tracks that would give me more to go on. Then, on my way home from the woods, I saw a couple walking a dog as big as a black bear. I stopped to talk to them and asked if they had been up in the snow with the dog. The dog's name, by the way, was Tiny and he came up to my car and put his head in my window without stretching up.

"Yes," they said, "We take Tiny up on the back roads for runs."

I looked down at Tiny's ungainly large paws. My wolf bubble burst.

~ The Punctuation in an Animal Trail ~

An animal sign that can lead you to tracks is where an animal has left a scat. They need to have paws on the ground to leave scat, so whenever I find, for instance, a bear scat in the road, I know there are bear tracks there too.

One of my first adventures in trailing a black bear started when I was riding my bike on a quiet back road and stopped to look at a large, huckleberry-filled, shining wet bear scat. I put my bike down and carefully approached the scat, which was sitting on a soft part of the gravel road. I couldn't see the bear tracks but I knew they must be there.

I circled the area until the light was just right for me to see them lightly etched in the dust. Surprisingly, the tracks showed that the bear was facing toward the right side of the road when it left the pile. I kept looking until I saw some more tracks, even less defined and only noticeable as I moved pebbles. I followed them to the side of the road where there were indistinct paw depressions in the grass; what I call "soft paw" tracks. Down the bank I could see a leaf turned over on a bush, showing the lighter underside.

I went down there and parted the brush to see if I could see more. There were a few bent-over weeds about twenty feet further down and I went that way. I was just thinking to myself that surely I had lost the trail when I came to a log about knee height. On top of the log was a fungus, or what was left of one. It was squashed and showing a clear bear track. The moisture was still running down the log, so I paused to look around. I didn't see the bear but I'm sure it saw me.

As I stood there, wondering if I dare go on, I heard a stick crack. I decided to back off at that point, but I was so happy I was able to trail the animal that far.

Mark Elbroch is the author of an excellent book called *Mammal Tracks & Sign,* which includes an extensive chapter on foot morphology and animal gaits. One of the reasons I draw or photograph tracks in the field is to confirm my findings later at home with the help of a good field guide. (You'll find my field guide recommendations in resources listed at the back of this book.) Drawing helps you remember to sort out the parts of a track, like how many digits and claw marks you see, what kind of a palm pad shows up, and if the track is a single print or a double register (when an animal steps in its own paw print). Sometimes double register can be hard to see if they're good at it. Look for a second set of ridges in the print. Other times, they do it in a sloppy manner and it looks like a track with six or more toes.

If you can find tracks in a trail pattern, the measurements of the stride and straddle will further help identify the animal and give you a clue to the gait the animal used to move. The gait of the animal then leads to what the animal was doing. Many field guides go over in great detail how to measure tracks.

Personally, I like the works of Dr. James Halfpenny for track measurements. Halfpenny discovered that there were discrepancies in field guides when it came to measurements, so he advocates a method of measuring from the inside wall of the track. Measuring consistently means more precise information.

Each animal I have learned about has taught me lessons about tracking. One of the main ones is that animals don't read the books about themselves. Their behavior changes as the world changes around them. When I hear, "That can't be a fox track. We don't have foxes here," I know it's definitely worth a second look, as animals go wherever they want to. For instance, for thirty years we haven't had doves at my house. Then one day, we did.

Taking classes, reading the tracking books, and spending time on your own out looking at the landscape will turn you into a tracker. Once you become intent on reading those "stories on the ground," where you can't seem to get enough of it, it's time for you to look up CyberTracker North America and sign up for a weekend evaluation.

The first time you do this, a whole new world will open up for you. The format they use to teach tracking is a test. Interestingly, any question you get wrong on an evaluation is something you will never, ever forget. So in failing, you win. If you know everything, you have nothing more to learn, but each evaluation I have been a part of has taught me more in two days than weeks of learning on my own.

Don't worry if you feel you don't know enough yet to take a test. One of the things that the CyberTracker system is good at, is alerting us to what it is that we don't know yet. We can't get there if we don't even know where we are going.

Then, if you haven't already done so, you will need to look into human tracking courses. Tracking humans is a great way to learn how to trail. In Africa, trailing and tracking are the same. In the U.S., tracking means identifying the animal by sign on the landscape but not necessarily following it. Which is what we call trailing.

~ Why Trailing? ~

Following an animal can offer incredible insight into their daily lives. Yesterday where Jane and I parked our cars to unload our bikes we noticed a big, black stinky and hairy animal scat in the middle of the road. As we walked up on it, we looked for tracks in the dusty gravel.

The light was dim and tracking was hard but we finally pieced together a couple of likely-looking spots where a soft-pawed animal had stood to deposit the scat. We measured the scat. Consensus between us was mountain lion. The indistinct tracks didn't rule that out. We slowly examined the dust in the road in both directions, sussing out some more feline-looking tracks with four toes that were as fresh as the scat. The flies were just finding the scat and the impressions of cat tracks were lightly etched in the soft dust. But there was a problem. Two of the tracks were side by side and cats just don't walk like that.

"Oh!" I said to Jane, "One of these is smaller!"

Down the road we went, picking out the occasional visible clue that the two animals went that way. When we got to an intersection, we found another scat just like the first one in color, age, contents, and placement on the road...only it was smaller.

The mystery got clearer. It was probably a female mountain lion, as evidenced by the size of her tracks and the fact that she was traveling with a smaller cat who had been eating the same things.

It made my day to figure these things out and get a glimpse into the lives of two special animals. It happened that Jane had seen an elk carcass a few days before on the other side of the hill. We spent some more time figuring out if the two animals had fed on that carcass and how many miles they traveled before leaving the scat.

These days, when people are starting to use trail cameras to find out more about animals, it seems like you could just skip learning to see all that subtle sign. But it is essential to finding a spot that works for a trail camera to be able to track and find locations where animals come and go on a regular basis and humans do not. Successful trail camera photographers are good trackers first.

Tracking and trailing skills also help you stay safe in the woods.

First, it's even harder to get lost when you know how to follow human sign. You can always follow yourself back out. Trackers don't need flagging tape.

Second, it is very helpful to know who else is in the area, and what they are doing there.

Once I was teaching a class near the Pacific Crest Trail. When we got to the area we wanted to track, we saw a car parked at the trailhead. One of the exercises I do is to ask students to examine, without touching it, a car and the ground around it to learn as much as they can about the people who drove it.

My class did a great job that day. They decided it was a man with a walking stick by himself, some kind of government worker or law enforcement. He was from Portland and had been there about an hour. They deduced he was probably carrying a gun. They noted a license plate holder that said, "Oregon Trust."

We went on up the trail and got caught up in animal sign, following a black bear that was turning over logs looking for grubs. When we heard a Douglas squirrel alarm up the trail, we remembered the man. We watched as he came by, walking with purpose with his hiking stick and looking surprised to see anyone else on the trail.

"So, what's the Oregon Trust?" I asked him when he nodded to us.

He stopped. He looked at me hard. "Why do you ask?"

"Oh, it's on your license plate."

"How do you know which car is mine?"

He was defensive by this time and looking quite angry as his hand dropped, probably unconsciously, to his gun.

I hastened to explain that we were a tracking class and had used his car to teach awareness since it was parked right on the trailhead. He still looked mad but he did admit to it being his car.

The class waited until he was well out of hearing range before they laughed and high-fived each other. They got it right enough for us all to recognize him at first glance. They also got the time right, as it takes two hours to hike that section of the trail and back.

It's a comfort when you are alone to know who is around and what they are doing. You can't know it all, of course, but you can get a good idea. Maybe it's from all my human tracking courses, but I never go up a trail or road without looking to see if someone else is there.

~6~

Scatology

Gross you say? Well, you're right. It's gross to go around looking at animal scat. However, it's a good way to start tracking. Animals don't think their scat is gross. On the contrary, they are often proud of the piles of poo they leave around.

Wild animals work hard to get their food. They plan, scheme and hunt diligently, and each meal is hard-won. Even if they are herbivores eating grass, they hunt and taste constantly to find the best, freshest, tastiest, and most tender plants.

Predators place their scat carefully, as the smellier they are, the more they have a message to send to other animals. Coyotes are sh*t artists, and become very creative in the placement of their scat. The middle of the road or trail suits them fine and even better if it is on top of a rock or a piece of wood.

Mark Elbroch's *Mammal Tracks & Sign: A Guide to North American Species* includes a pretty complete array of color scat photos, as well as descriptions. It's a good place to start.

Some of the general rules about scatology are that measuring the scat helps. You want an idea of the total length, the diameter, and the contents. To understand the contents, sometimes you will have to use a stout stick and break apart the scat. This, of course, should be done carefully, and after you take any photographs and measurements. (As a side note, several times we have come across disturbed scat and knew another tracker had been there. Be conscious of ruining the sign for others, and don't delve into a scat if you don't have to.)

There are a few things I use to determine species when I find scat. One of them is the placement of the scat.

Like I mentioned, coyotes tend to be creative. Once I almost fell off my bike when I rounded a corner and found a squashed beer can in the middle of the road with a hairy, twisted, tapered fresh coyote scat placed right on top of the can with one of the tapered ends sticking up in the air. It looked like the coyote was giving whoever left the can the finger. Maybe he was mad that there was none left for him. More likely, he was elevating his scat so the scent would pass on down the trail in the wind to advertise his hunting abilities and his or her presence.

Diameter of the scat is also something I look at.

Sometimes, like when a certain berry crop is filling the air with aroma and the bushes are loaded, all the animals eat the same thing for a few days. Then the trail is loaded with scat that looks the same in texture and contents. The only difference is the shape and diameter.

I tell my classes this, so I might as well type it here. When you are trying to decide who left the scat, just picture the asshole that left it. Is it wide like a bear, or narrow like a fisher (a North American mammal)?

In the *Mammal Tracks & Sign* book I mentioned above, Mark Elbroch puts this in a more scientific context: "Scat diameters (the widths) are more reliably diagnostic because the dimension is mainly predetermined by the internal excretory structures of the animal responsible."

(Thanks Mark. It's a much nicer way of saying it.)

Bobcats and coyotes leave close to the same size scats because they are very similar in overall size. Canine scat is generally twisted and tapered, whereas bobcat is often sectioned and smooth, looking more like a cigar with blunt ends. Bobcats sometimes leave a scent scrape nearby and canines sometimes do a little ritual with their back legs where they swipe the ground as if cleaning their paws which throws material out behind.

Cougars leave a bigger diameter and quantity of scat, but it looks similar to bobcat. It's also dense and sometimes it has a dark covering. The first cougar scat I ever saw looked like a black tree limb. Density can be determined by your stout stick and giving the scat a little pressure.

Determining the age of the scat is also important. Is it marinating in a pool of pee, or is it dry and white, indicating that it's been there awhile? In spring, old scat can look fresh if it has just melted out of snow. A new scat will have flies or butterflies on it.

If it's new, that also means that you should be able to find the associated tracks there. Picture the animal making the scat and look for paw prints. If you can tell which way the animal was facing, you will have a trailing opportunity.

Frog scats are amazingly large in size. They are full of bug bodies, though. Turkey scats are sort of like chicken scats, but some of them are super gooey and smelly. The grossest scat to me is marten or weasel. I once put my hand in marten scat by accident. Now I never sit on a log perch without looking first.

When a bird sh*ts on your car, make a habit of determining what they are eating. Is it bugs, berries, or seeds? Gross, but you'll get some local information out of it.

In the long run, you can learn a lot about the lives of animals by the stuff they leave behind. Scat, discarded nests, dens, and pellets can give the astute observer a look into how the animal lives and what parts of the habitat are important for that animal. Then, if you study for a few years, you can start to make the connections of time of year for certain foods.

For instance, bears have a yearly menu. Depending on where they live, that might look like this:

Just out of the den
Winter kill or left over smelly carcasses
Early spring
Green-up in the lower elevations of the area in which they live
Early summer
Following the green-up back up the hill or mountain
Mid summer
Fish runs or spawned-out fish
Late summer
Berry season, in the order that the berries get ripe
Fall
Mast, or nuts and seeds of trees and anything they can find to build fat

Raccoon scat is dangerous. They create latrines that more than one animal uses and it can be in an elevated place. Don't poke around in raccoon scat or breathe its dust. Humans can catch some nasty diseases from them. Raccoon scat can also be mistaken for bear scat as they often eat the same things. When more than one animal deposits in the same spot, it can look like a big bear pile.

Now that you know a bit more about it, you can post your scat photos on social media and all your non-tracking friends will think you have really gone batty.

~ 7 ~

Trailing Animals—and Humans

I'm going to spend some time on the skill of trailing here, as not many tracking books cover it. When anything moves on the landscape it leaves what trackers call "sign." Sign, as it relates to tracking, is a noun, and covers everything from footprints to subtle brushed-aside leaves. You can see sign or disturbance in any substrate; yes, including on asphalt roads and cement floors.

To start your journey into this kind of awareness, you can start tracking yourself.

Go to a place where other people haven't walked recently and leave a line of sign for yourself. Put a marker on the ground, a stone, a flag or something where you started and walk to a place about fifty yards away. Put a marker on the ground at your end spot that you can't see from your starting point. Walk well around to get back to your starting point.

It isn't easy to remember exactly where you walked. When you find your beginning marker look at the first tracks you made carefully. Notice what happened to the small stuff on the ground when you stepped on it. By following yourself, you can learn what to look for in various substrates. After thirty years of trailing myself, I still have things to learn. There's always a new substrate to experiment with. What kind of sign do you leave on sand, gravel, grass, the golf course, or the living room rug?

The by-product of this exercise is that you become aware of when you are leaving tracks and when you're not. After a while, you know what to step on and how to leave a good trail. If you purposely squash a mushroom, you'll remember that if you need to find your way back out. If you break a branch on a bush and leave it hanging and swinging in the wind, you'll see that when you go that way again. Like I mentioned before, trackers usually don't need flagging tape, even to find their trail cameras deep in the woods.

I took classes from several different kinds of schools for trailing experience. I always thought it was worthwhile to go to a class where expert trackers laid sign for the students all weekend long. Trailing schools teach teamwork and, even though I like to track alone, teamwork is necessary and more efficient in certain situations.

The search and rescue crews teach step-by-step tracking because when human lives are at stake, you cannot make a mistake. Step by step is the same exercise I gave you, but the sign is laid by expert trackers who want you to look deeply into every track so you learn how to be precise in your tracking by learning every little detail of what things look like when they are stepped on by humans. Humans leave sharp edges that animals don't, and they leave telltale characteristics in the way they move that signal their intentions.

Good human trackers possess interpretive skills built up over years of experience. It might seem like they are quoting out of the "Book of Tracking Bullsh*t" (more on that later) when they say a subject is in a panic and getting irrational, based on the tracks. But they can tell that and much more, just by the way a person walks and where they go.

Another way to teach trailing humans comes from the tactical side. Law enforcement and soldiers use these skills. One method is to divide the class into teams. Five people head out on the trail, walking single file, and the second team follows them, all the while expecting to be ambushed. If the trailing (second) team walks right into the first group unaware, they are "dead." If they are able to locate the first team and sneak up on them, then the trailing team "wins." Then the teams trade places and the trailing team sets off to set up an ambush.

As the class progresses, the teams get smaller until they are trailing one person, which is danged hard. There are times when lives are dependent on the skill of the tracker. Staying alive as a motivation for learning it is huge.

One of the exercises I do in my classes is less crucial. I go out on a walk in the woods and I leave pieces of flagging tape in my tracks once in a while. I usually have two teams working the sign and when they come across a tape piece, they change teams and the second one takes the lead. I call this the chocolate trail because I leave wrapped chocolate kisses in purple wrappers in places in plain sight. I usually get to eat all the chocolate because my students get so focused on the trail, they forget to look up. It's not as punitive as looking for an ambush up ahead, but it has a similar effect.

When I teach beginning students, I start them on an easy trail that my assistant Jane and I leave for them. They are frequently surprised that they can see a trail in a place where they would never expect to be able to follow someone.

This is a skill that anyone can learn; it just takes practice and the desire to do it. Once you learn to see trails and tracks, however, you will never not see them. Walking with a tracker can keep you safe from stepping on things like snakes and gum and icky things.

When someone says "there weren't any tracks," a red flag should go up. That's only part of the information. The question is, were there no tracks because the elements effectively removed them, i.e., blowing sand or snow? Or, did the reporting party just assume there were no tracks because an untrained eye couldn't see them?

The "no tracks" statement can be completely misunderstood.

One night during the Christmas season, a boy was reported lost in Oregon. He had been out getting a Christmas tree with family and they reported that when it was time to leave, they couldn't find him. There was a search callout and a team from Oregon responded.

The trackers were the first at the place where the reporting party said they last saw the little boy. They didn't find any tracks. They reported to the deputies in charge of the search by radio that there were no tracks. A news reporter misinterpreted the statement, assuming that the trackers just couldn't see the tracks. I'm not sure if the deputy also interpreted it that way, but they sent more teams and looked for days. The local Portland newspaper lambasted the team, claiming incompetence, insinuating that the team Christmas party was more important than the little boy. The fact was, though, that the tracking team meant what they said. There were no tracks. The reporting party had not even been there. Years later, it came to light that the whole search was an insurance scam and the tracking team was right on. There were literally no tracks.

Or, the statement can mean that there were no tracks because the reporting person thought you can't see tracks in grass, gravel, or on cement, etc., so they didn't look for tracks.

One night my rescue pack was stolen from my car, which was unlocked but in our garage. The thief also broke into Mike's woodshop by prying open a door. They took some tools.

I was really upset about my pack, as I had about a thousand dollars' worth of personal gear in there that wouldn't be easy to replace.

I called the Sheriff's office and they sent a deputy to my house. He took a statement and told me that there had been a few thefts in the area and they were working on it. He left.

I did a tour of the dumpsters in the area, thinking whoever it was might have taken the good stuff and then discarded the pack. To no avail.

It was raining and cool. I came home and drank a second cup of coffee and then I remembered my lessons from human tracking classes. No one had looked for tracks. I guess they thought no one would be able to see them because there wasn't a clear substrate like mud, snow, dust, or sand.

Our back yard was full of leaf litter and squishy mud, with the brown leaves in layers. I knew no one in my house had been back there for a day or so, so I looked. Amazingly the first boot print was pretty clear. It was leaving the garage, just off the end of the sidewalk that extended along the garage. I got some flagging tape and pulled off a little piece and marked the track. Then I found the next one. Pretty soon, I had a picture in my mind of what the tracks looked like in that substrate and was able to piece together a trail, dropping tape in each track I found to be able to show the trail to someone else if I needed to. (Flagging tape or colored popsickle sticks are good for training or working in forensics tracking, where you need to preserve the trail.)

The trail led me out of our yard to the neighbors' shed, and then on to another neighbor's shed where the tracks seemed to stop.

I was standing there staring intently at the ground to see where the person had gone from there, when the neighbor, whose land I was on, came out of his house to see what I was doing. I explained to him about the thief and showed him the line of tracks.

He said it was his shed and he had the key, "So let's just open it up and see what's in there."

He fumbled with the key but couldn't get the lock to open. Finally he realized someone had changed the lock. He went to his garage and got a crowbar.

When we got the door open, not only was my rescue pack in there, so were a lot of other cool things that had recently gone missing. I called the deputies on my cell phone and they came right out.

The thief turned out to be the son of the shed owner and some of his friends who needed money for drugs.

So the lesson is, never think that you won't be able to see tracks somewhere unless you try. Being able to trail and see sign is a very worthwhile skill to have.

~ Subtle Things to Look For When Trailing ~

pushed down vegetation

broken flowers

runner plants pulled up off the ground

squashed mushrooms or fungi

broken fir or pine cones

swirled fir or pine needles

depressions in the soil or mud

rock cavities where rocks have been kicked out

rocks with new shadows around them where they have been pushed in

dirt or dust on the rocks from the surrounding soils

water droplets where a wet animal went through dry vegetation

dry vegetation where an animal went through and knocked the water off

turned-over leaves

broken sticks on brush

broken sticks on the ground

a three-way broken stick where a step pushed down the middle part

spider webs broken (although they rebuild within the hour)

dirt transfer from muddy boots or paws on rocks, downed trees, or vegetation

moss brushed off trees

fur on brush, fences, or snagged by briars

~ From *Lonesome for Wilderness* ~

~ And the Big Things to Look For, Always ~

scent marking scrapes in the dirt, on downed logs or forest duff

scent marking on trees with claws, fur, and chews

animal beds in long grass, on hillsides or in forest duff

nests, dens

scats of all animals and pee spots

a line of clear animal prints in mud, dust, snow, and puddles

antler rubs

bee nests

cambium layer feeding on trees

digging spots for small mammals and bugs

dead trees with tear marks where animals are seeking bugs

kill sites and cache sites; bones and skulls

pellets from birds

feeding sign of browsing animals

ant hills and other insect nests predated by animals

feathers

holes of all sizes and attitudes where animals live

harvested vegetation saved for later

runs in grass and brush from small mammals

trails deeply cut into the substrate from animal re-use over time

bear stomp trails

~ From *Lonesome for Wilderness* ~

You can learn a lot about humans and animals by learning to trail. Once I trailed a couple of hunters down a back road. I first determined that they had been there the night before and where they had parked. Their trail showed me that they were tracking a big bull elk. I wanted to see if they got it, so I kept following them.

Their boot prints had left a really easy trail because the mud was wet and it was full of clay. It was drier the day after they went through when I was walking their trail, but I could see that their boots collected the mud and dropped it off as they walked. (Trackers call this dirt transfer). The elk seemed to lead them in a straightforward manner down the curving road and I wondered why it didn't take evasive action as the hunters couldn't have been quiet, the way they were walking. After a sharp corner, the road suddenly stopped at a wall of small alder trees growing in the road bed.

The stalks of the little trees were so close together that it didn't seem like you could walk through them, certainly not if you had a big rack of antlers. The hunters milled around at that spot and then headed up the hill into the woods on an animal trail that would take them in the direction their truck was parked. I started to follow them and noticed the elk tracks were gone. I went back to the last elk track.

"Huh."

I didn't think the elk flew out of there, so I kept looking for the next track in that spot but darned if I could see it. I walked around in a circle and looked...nothing. The only place left was the wall of alder trees.

Finally, I got down on the ground and found it. Something had gone through there. I pushed aside some of the trees and squeezed in. The marks on the ground were not elk tracks though. I looked at the sign and then rocked back on my heels. Danged if it wasn't the knees and leg marks of the elk. The elk crawled through on its knees! It broke a few branches inside but the leg marks showed me how to follow it. In about twenty yards the alders stopped and the elk stood up. I was able to follow him into a meadow wetlands from there, but of course, his tracks were also from the day before, so I didn't get to see him.

Trailing is most fun when you can put together the signs left behind and tell which way the live thing went, and/or came from. and when.

"When?" is the clue you need most to actually find the trail-maker. In tracking we call that aging the sign. In other words, sorting out the signs on the ground into who was here first and who was the last to pass by. In search and rescue, sometimes you need to sort the three-day-old sign that was most likely left by the lost subject, from the stuff that is left the day you are looking. I've noticed that trackers who cook understand the concept of freshness if you tell them to look at it like they would a salad. Is the lettuce fresh and the vegetables freshly cut? Any chef, male or female, can master aging.

So, you see a deer cross the trail up ahead of you and you want to follow it and see where it goes. First, you have to find the track in the trail, because judging distance when you see an animal cross in front of you is hard. When you find it, even if it is only a scuff mark, it will be fresher than any other sign on the trail. It might be on top of a boot print. It could be just a spot where the leaves got kicked up slightly. Then stand there quietly and look slowly around. Don't just look where you think it came from but look at everything. Then, see if you can see where it went. Perhaps there is a leaf turned showing a pale green underside, or a broken stick on a bush the animal brushed by. It could be that the hooves registered by pushing down vegetation, breaking a sharp ridge into the soil that you can feel with your fingers but can't see. You might be able to see an entire line of sign by what trackers call "shine." Because when all the leaves and brush are pushed through by a body, it can show a slightly different color to the careful observer. This color difference might be in the "top sign," which is off the ground, or on the ground itself if you're lucky.

If you detect the direction the animal went, follow the trail, moving slowly but steadily while taking note of the details. To find the animal, you'll need to learn to do this out of the corner of your eye while you look ahead and up. If you find a small broken branch, you can feel it as you go by to check on the age of the sign you are following. When several trails intersect, the only way through is to detect the most recent sign.

If you need to drop down to feel the ground, keep your eyes up and simply glance down briefly. Let your fingers discover the freshness of stirred up soil or broken-down vegetation.

It might take a while for you to learn to do this, but the rewards are definitely worth the effort. The first time you trail a deer to where it stopped to graze after crossing the trail, nobody will be able to rain on your parade for a long time. Deer can teach you a lot about life.

~ 8 ~

Changing Habitats

The signs of life in the world are all connected, like a knitted sweater. If one of the threads hits a snag and gets pulled, the whole thing can unravel but the yarn is still there. Patterns can be rebuilt but they will be different. What's there now will evolve. This is true for all kinds of different habitats, from deserts to deep forests.

In order to be a good tracker, you need to change too. One of the best ways to practice changing your outlook is to experience a wholly different ecosystem.

Every year when my husband and I migrate to Baja California, I start exploring a completely different system of life. I go from mossy stumps shaded by thick canopy, to sandy beaches and hardpan desert floors with mesas and a completely different set of plant life. The skill of noticing disturbances stays with you but there are new animals, and different versions of the ones you've learned.

One year, while we were camped on the Pacific Ocean, I saw a clear line of tracks going through our camp in the dewy sand. It was a four-toed animal that wasn't showing claw marks and the metacarpal pad had three dots on the bottom edge. My first thought was that it was a domestic cat. I followed the trail for a mile and determined that the tracks were a consistent one-and-a-half inches wide. In my experience at the time, domestic kitties left tracks of an inch or under. Wild bobcat tracks are around two inches wide in the Pacific Northwest. I was mystified.

It's always more difficult to think out a problem when you don't have another tracker to bounce things off, who won't think you are an idiot for not knowing answers. It took me a long time to answer my own questions. I used a trail camera and an empty tuna can set up on a fence line where I had seen the same tracks. I finally got a picture of the little twerp! It was indeed a bobcat.

I learned that bobcats in Baja are smaller and they have less fur on their paws. Hence the different-looking tracks. A hard lesson, but one that has come back to help me many times. The deer in Baja are smaller, and the coyotes as well. The desert animals work harder for their food and need to move more often.

It has been really fun to learn about desert animals, as each place we camp on our way down the peninsula hosts a different community of animals interacting in unique ways. The jack rabbits stand as big as a midsize dog and the spiders cast long shadows. Tarantulas seem to walk to music and hermit crabs drag their shells off-balance, which creates interesting patterns. Bones lie around for years and you can find intact skulls to study. The wind uncovers whale bones and the tide takes out layers of sand, which exposes full skeletons of sea life.

The beach and the desert, being side by side, yield astounding mysteries and interconnections. For instance, I always thought great blue herons waded in the shallows and ate fish. One day I watched one moving around in the dry grasses among sand dunes. I kept wondering what the heck it was doing. Then, it pecked hard at the ground and I saw the head come up with a wiggling mouse tail sticking out of its beak.

"Oh yeah," I told myself. "That heron didn't read that bird book, huh?"

~ Puzzles ~

I ran into a tracking friend in a Baja restaurant one evening who wanted me to look at a new track he'd found. He pulled out his phone and encouraged me to scroll through a few pictures. It brought back a vivid memory for me and I smiled.

I remembered a beach near the Sea of Cortez where I found what I thought were mountain bike tracks. I spotted a continuous pattern in the sand, winding around. Only, it wound around too tightly to actually be a bike. "Huh." So I followed it to its home, where I found one of the many species of crabs that run around on the beach down there.

My friend was stymied like I had been. He wasn't the only person who brought me phone photos of the same kind of track. We're all clueless, until we're not.

I can stare into a tide pool for hours, or at least until the tide comes back in and chases me away. I've learned that the animals in a tide pool are pretty aware when a human looks into the pool. They hide. The only way you can really see what is there is to put yourself in a spot to watch where they can't sense your shadow and you don't move for a while. If you can stay there long enough, the magic happens. The octopus comes out and tries to find your feet, or a bird of prey sneaks up and grabs a crab. The snails crawl around and the little fish dart out, look around, and leave a swirl of sand when they depart.

Trailing animals in the desert of Baja is much easier than forest tracking in some ways. Clear tracks can show you the way but to catch up with the animal, you need to have a deep understanding of the habitat and what it offers in the way of food, water, and shelter for the animal you seek. Knowing where the elusive fresh water drips down secluded rocks, and where certain lush plants flourish in shaded little box canyons, can steer you as much as the tracks and sign. The weather and the time of day are also key. Certain spots become active in the afternoon or morning shade. Even the range cattle in Baja follow patterns of ease in their daily wanderings. They know where to drink and where people throw their yard debris and at what stage a house construction site might yield the ever-popular empty cement bags, which they love to chew on for some mineral left in them.

There are wild burros and herds of goats wandering in the hills, as well. Sometimes you can hear the bells of goats and cattle for a long way. Sometimes they have guard dogs with them, with unpredictable behavior when it comes to humans.

In Baja, the domestic animal shares a different relationship with humans than our farm animals in the U.S. do. Many of them are left to fend for themselves for months at a time. Traditionally, dogs are dogs in Mexico, not fur babies. Although this trend is changing, don't expect pet-like behavior from any animal in Mexico.

When night comes, the hunters come out. The scorpions leave the safe cracks in the rocks and set up an ambush. A tracker with a black light can spot them hanging out from fifty feet away. Like most species I was formerly afraid of, learning the habits of scorpions made me like and appreciate them. They are shy animals and the sound of a human voice will send them scurrying for cover. Discovering one of them eating a cockroach further endeared them to me.

For a few weeks, I watched one scorpion I called Heidi, as she came out to hunt at night and hid deep in a stone wall during the day. The way to get stung is to step on one, have it hide in your shoe or clothes, or reach into a dark place without looking. A walk on the beach at night (I recommend sandals) with a blacklight, a flashlight, and in the dark exposes an amount of life you might have thought during the day did not exist in this place.

Life in the desert is accessible and incredibly varied. Last winter I found a set of tracks in the sand that took me a long time to identify. It was a two-inch wide trail with the weirdest markings I have ever seen. I went through every field guide, all the online references for trackers, and could not come up with an answer that was in any way satisfying. To make it worse, the animal came back and left more tracks while I was sleeping.

Finally, I resorted to posting pictures of the tracks on one of the track study groups for CyberTracker. I wasn't the only one who didn't recognize the tracks of a big...*really* big centipede. It took a tracker from Israel to clue me in to the track maker. (Journal sketch p. 13.)

Even a large cardon cactus makes a big impact on the area it's in. Cactus species are the masters of holding water. The ridges on a cardon expand when the plant collects moisture and contract slowly as it gets thirsty. They live for hundreds of years and serve as hosts to animals.

You might see a hole in a stout cardon cactus, indicating a

cavity big enough for an owl family to live in. Bobcats sometimes perch on the top of them.

The flora of the desert might look uninteresting at first glance, but a winding walk through the choya, mesquite bushes, sage, and thorny things you can't identify will show you a close interaction between the bugs, animals, and plants. Coming from northern forests, a person might feel deprived and lonely at first, but the desert grows on you. After a while, just like in the forest, you can't look anywhere without seeing signs of the fascinating survival behaviors of many species.

Even though I miss the bears, cougars, and wolves of the Northwest, the desert is rich with intrigue and drama. Packs of coyotes sing on the mesa tops while whales swim below them. Badgers cover huge territories where mice, kangaroo rats, pack rats, and antelope ground squirrels make for fat badgers. Birds of prey include the Crested Caracara, a predatory bird that displays stylish markings. Owls, ravens, and hawks benefit from migrating smaller birds and a proliferation of bugs.

And everywhere in the desert there are holes, from the cones of ant lions to dens for packs of coyotes. A great little field guide, *Desert Holes* by Pinau Merlin, helped me find answers about them. It's full of illustrations,and color photos and can easily fit in a pack.

One winter I was traveling light in Baja with a friend when I met a woman on one of the popular Sea of Cortez beaches who was collecting a fuzzy white ant from the sand. We started a conversation and she told me that she was traveling alone in her truck camper, studying bugs. The one she collected while I watched was a "nurse ant" or fire ant, a hard-biting, fast little bug with beautiful white fur.

The woman interested me because she traveled alone, and because she told me that she had been a biologist in Canada, working with large animals. Now, as she aged, she started studying bugs because, "They are the only thing I can still catch."

I was comforted by the thought that, no matter how old you get, you can still study nature. That will be me, out in the woods in my wheelchair or on a remote beach camped by the tide pools, putting numbers on the backs of snails and watching them race.

~ 9 ~

Lions and Bears

Fear is a funny thing. It can kill you, or save you. In some cases, you can fear the least dangerous thing around, only to be killed by something you never would have thought of. Like a slippery rock in a creek bed that causes you to fall…and go over the downstream falls.

I grew up terrified of black bears. Well, any bears, but black bears lived in my state and the only thing I ever heard about them was that they were dangerous and unpredictable and would attack with huge teeth and claws and rip you to bits. Telling scary bear stories was a thing back then. Scalps ripped off and bears eating people alive. You know, stuff big brothers have fun telling you.

Then there was the story, told by a friend, of a guy camping in a tent and hearing something rummaging around in camp. He looked out and saw a black bear, but he thought most of the food was in the car, so he went back to sleep. A while later, he was woken up by a bear licking his face with a peanut butter coated tongue.

Ah yes, those horrifying stories. Funny how you never forget them.

~ Bears ~

In my quest for safety in the woods, I had to ask the question. Are bears really dangerous? This question became vital after I was on a bike ride in the forest by myself and encountered a bear.

I was sitting by the trail eating an apple and looking at the map. When I stood up to move on, a black bear burst out of the bushes right by my bike, flew across the road, and took off down into the valley. It made a lot of noise. I was startled and watched with my mouth open as the wind from its passage washed over me and I noticed the blue-black, shiny hair rippling with muscles. My adrenalin spiked and my hands shook.

I think I said out loud, "Am I in danger here?"

No one answered, so I got on my bike and rode away as fast as I could. I ran into some hikers down the trail and sputtered that I had seen a bear!

They acted like it was no big deal.

It was a big deal to me. Such a big deal that I put my bike in the garage and thought I wouldn't do that again. "That" being riding by myself.

After about ten days of staying home because no one wanted to ride with me, I got mad about giving up the new freedom I had been enjoying so much. That's when I set out to learn.

I started with books from the library on bears. They ranged from horror stories to Tim Treadwell's tales of furry friends others called grizzly bears. The truth was elusive, ranging from being dragged out of your tent and eaten, to people raising and feeding "pet" bears.

Reading about bears led me to some books about tracking. I checked out books on the subject and read the amazing stories of Tom Brown. I borrowed field guides to tracks and studied books from Paul Rezendes and Jim Halfpenny. I got on a primitive tracker's forum online. I still know some of the trackers from that early forum, some thirty-five years later.

After reading all I could find and soaking up any information I could get about tracking, I went back to the spot where the bear had run past me earlier that summer. With a newfound interest in being a nature detective, I discovered that I had chosen to take my break on a well-worn bear path. When I walked the trail that the bears use, coming down on the spot where I had been sitting, I guessed that the bear had been as surprised as I was, and probably just as scared.

The more I learned about bears, the more fascinated I became. They are the coolest characters. They live a life of looking for food and comfort, and they're very good at it. They aren't inherently mean or aggressive, and each bear is different, just like dogs are different.

My tracking journey led me to get a job in Alaska at a bear-viewing lodge with my husband Mike. Because I had a boat captain's license and Mike had hotel management skills, we were hired as co-managers for a fly-in only resort. Mike was in charge of the land-based operations and I was head guide, in charge of the boats and guides.

Who would have thought that I could go from feeling terrified of bears (to the point where I wouldn't have minded if they were all killed), to really liking these furry characters and showing them to other people? For four summers, I got to hang out with black bears and grizzly/brown bears almost every day. Bears taught me a lot about all animals.

Being close to bears is an incredible experience. They

communicate in body language with each other and with us, if we take time to notice. They are emotional geniuses and can read you in a nanosecond. Because they don't crowd their brain with verbal language, they are open to ways of communicating we probably can't even imagine.

All I know, from working with them so much, is that they are not stupid. They have lots of feelings and emotions and lead rich lives in the natural world that we only see a surface view of. They form complex relationships with each other and with other animals as well. They play, they chase each other and sometimes disagree, but they never seem to seriously hurt one another.

Female bears have a cool system called delayed implantation, which controls the population. When they mate in the spring, a group of cells called a blastocyst form in the uterus but do not attach to the uterus wall to become cubs unless the mother gets fat enough and healthy enough to have cubs during her hibernation. If the habitat is poor, the mothers won't have cubs, thereby managing their own population.

I got to watch mother bears adopt orphans, and the drama on the days when it was finally time for the cubs to go their own way.

Mother bears teach the cubs when and how to eat the multitude of foods that can be found in the area. The tender new shoots of certain plants come at different times and a good mother bear passes that information down to the cubs. The cubs follow their mothers closely and when she finds something good to eat, they put their tongues in the mother's mouth to taste it too. Their mothers teach them how to avoid natural dangers and how to pick and build a hibernation spot.

Grizzly bear mothers keep their cubs for two summers and black bears keep them for one.

One of the reasons spring bear hunts are so detrimental to both humans and bears, is that the cubs who are orphaned by accident don't get an education on how to be a bear. These cubs must resort to any behavior, no matter how brazen, to get food and survive, which is often at odds with human needs. If a female orphan bear has cubs, those new behaviors are passed on to another generation. Human/bear coexistence could be improved if we let wild bears teach their offspring how to stay wild.

Another reason spring bear hunts can quickly diminish a population is that is the time when sub-adult (read teenage) bears are newly separated from their mothers and on their own for the first time. Like human teenagers, they still don't have enough wisdom to guide them yet and might do some nitwit things like walk right up to a human…maybe on a dare from a sibling.

I've watched teenage bears get into trouble, and sometimes I wonder if they would just love to put their tongue into a human's mouth to see what we have been eating. The good news about teenage bears is that although they can be bold, they are also easy to scare.

As you can probably tell, the answer to my original question, "Are bears dangerous," is complicated. They are powerful, large animals with sharp claws and teeth and four-wheel drive that takes them quickly or slowly through any terrain. They all climb trees if they want and swim very well. But some of them are also downright sweet. They help each other and even other animals.

They might even help a human, if their actions weren't quickly misunderstood.

To animals we must appear to be crass, crash-about clumsy, loud, and stinky. It's possible that they think we are great hunters, though, because of the way we smell like rich food. When they try to talk to us, we just act weird. We run, scream, and or we approach them with this big metal thing with a huge eye (camera) and shove it in their face. Or, we just kill them if they move. I can't imagine what books about humans would be like if animals wrote them. We are monsters. No doubt about it.

When an animal finds a human who is peaceful and quiet and not making threatening moves, then a great encounter might unfold. This is true with any animal, from an insect to a wild elephant.

The best way to be around animals safely is to remain mindful, and care.

Not to push through that brush like a tank, not to run and yell, not to have a huge fire and lots of lights.

The more you place yourself as natural in nature, the better you can observe. An observant person is much safer from everything the earth has to offer, from poisonous plants to animals that might hurt you.

On the other end of that spectrum, if you, or someone you are with, accidentally find yourself in a place where you are standing on the ground near a seriously pissed-off animal, then there is another way to handle it.

Your instincts might tell you to run, and maybe scream, but that is the last thing you want to do. Good guides in Africa stand their ground and let the animal go ahead and have a tantrum. Showing weakness can get you killed. For instance, have you ever seen a little kitten stand off a big dog? It is the unwillingness to give in that wins.

Unless we are taught differently, it's easy for a human to accidentally appear rude or threatening to animals.

We cut tree limbs if they are in our way, rearranging the furniture in several animals' homes in the process.

We make fires, burning up the bugs that are an animal's food.

We park our cars on their scent trails.

We pee and poop on their food, and we pitch tents and drive nails into trees to hang our towels.

We walk into their house like we own it, and everything in it is just for our use.

Humans abuse as much of the woods as they feel like, then go home, usually not bothering to pick up after themselves. Staying aware of the signs, of the trails, tracks, scent marks, and the ways animals use their home can make your presence much less abrasive.

If you are alone, or with a small group of like-minded, quiet people who are willing to let nature magic unfold, then you are not only much safer, you are much rewarded with wildlife experiences.

It took several summers of watching bears before I appreciated their lessons to me. Since I was busy working as a guide and always had other people with me, it took a while for me to notice.

My first teacher was a mother brown bear with cubs that the guides called Baylee the summers I spent with her. She showed me a lot. But one day she kept looking at me intently. We were anchored in a small boat in the cove where people could watch bears pick spawning salmon out of a stream.

Baylee was sitting on one of her favorite rocks at the water's edge with her cubs. She was probably fifty feet from me, and she singled me out to stare at.

At first, I was uncomfortable with this situation and I kept glancing away, as that was what I had learned to do to de-escalate situations with bears. Then I gave up, and looked back at her, trying to understand what it was she wanted.

As soon as I did that, she huffed at her cubs who sat down on the spot, and she took off. The cubs, looking nervous with big rolling eyes, didn't move. They would glance at me and then look where their mother had gone. After a while, they lay down on the rock even though they were still jumpy.

An hour or so later, Baylee came back and gathered them up with gentle huffing and took them away. As she did so, she glanced meaningfully at me.

That was only the first time I was asked to babysit. The mothers in the cove used any guide with whom they could make mental contact to "keep" their cubs for a while.

The biologists assigned to record bear behavior in the area would admit privately that was what the bears were doing but in their research notes, they probably noted that bears who were accustomed to people sometimes used them to shield their cubs from other predators. Which is a less anthropomorphic way of saying the same thing.

The communications between species in a situation like this is easily ignored by humans. We are taught not to notice animals in that way. However, if you can slow down enough, your experience with animals could be amazing.

As a guide, once I learned to watch bears for visual clues, I also noticed that they expressed different reactions to the people I brought to see them. By watching closely, I could see who they liked and who made them nervous. There was usually a reason, and sometimes I even found out what it was.

Once I had a bear who kept swimming close to my boat seemingly for the sole purpose of giving the evil eye to one of my passengers. I didn't mention it or point it out to my group, but when they were getting on the plane to return home I said to the man, "You've been around bears before?"

"Oh yes," he said, "I've been hunting them for years."

That revelation made me wonder just how much bears can learn about people from observing us. I also wondered how many years of observation it would take for humans to understand them.

~ So, What Should You Do When You See a Bear? ~

Stop whatever you are doing and observe.

Remember that if you see one, it is probably an accident on the bear's part, because their senses are so acute, they can detect and avoid humans very well. Unless a bear wants to be seen, it usually isn't.

So if you do see one, the bear will be trying to make decisions about what to do, just like you are. You can assure it that you aren't about to kill it by glancing away casually. That's what they do with each other.

If the bear does the same, pretending it doesn't see you or glancing to the side, then you are golden. You can each move away from the encounter with ease. Move slowly and with your personal power out of sight. Moving sideways, instead of backwards, seems to work if you can get out of sight that way.

I know the standard advice is to wave your arms and yell to let the bear know you are human, and to stand your ground. If I were out in the woods and came upon a bear who stood up and waved its paws while making loud noises, I would seriously wonder if it was sane. So that advice probably works because no animal wants to deal with a crazy one.

If you get a chance to watch bears you can become comfortable with them. The next step is assuring them you aren't a threat in bear body language.

If you encounter a bear who has been fed and who is pushing you to feed it, you can downright save its life by hazing it. A few steps forward and a slap of your hand on your thigh, with a, "Don't even think about it buddy; my whole body is a weapon!"

If possible, a good dose of pepper spray could teach a bear that humans are as bad as skunks, or maybe worse. That could save a bear's life for sure.

It's interesting that the saying "a fed bear is a dead bear" has gone around so long. What it means is that if you intentionally or accidentally feed a bear, that bear will have to be killed. The reason stated is that once they taste human food, they are addicted and will become aggressive to get it.

Because bears are so smart, they can be trained. Hunters use bait stations of human food and garbage to catch bears on their trail cams and to lure bears into a spot where they can kill them. Then the bear stumbles onto a farm or campground and expects that any food left out is for him. However, a person can show bears that not all food left out is okay to eat. If they get disciplined with body language or pepper spray, they'll learn quickly.

The only time I ever had to use pepper spray on a bear was when a bear got into the dirty laundry at the lodge that was waiting to be flown out on the floatplane. The bear was having a fun time inside the holding shed, pulling the linen table cloths out of the bag. He couldn't be bothered that guides were trying to haze it out of the shed. This is because once they sink their teeth into something good, they consider it theirs. Possession is the rule of law in the bear world.

To teach a bear not to touch your food, it's best if you catch it before it samples a bite. It's still possible to get it to let go and move, but it's harder.

So I walked into the shed, brushed past the bear in the narrow space, and held my nose. I think I said something like, "Hey buddy, this is going to hurt me too." I let out a stream of pepper spray and the bear dug in his nails on the floor and went flying out of the shed as fast as he could go. I held my breath and exited too, just in time to see the bear well down the trail, headed away. I don't think that one ever came back.

Personally, I'm always hoping to see a bear. I even go so far as to trail them when I find fresh bear sign, learning about their lives and yearning to catch a glimpse of them without disturbing them too much.

My most recent bear encounter was with a mother bear and three second-year black bear cubs. I was on my electric bike, which is quiet, traveling alone down a grassy back road in Washington state when I rounded a corner and saw the group of black bears standing in the middle of the road.

I stopped and got off my bike. The cubs scrambled up a Douglas fir tree and the mother stayed on the ground. I felt bad that I had scared them, so I took the camp chair off my bike and sat down where I was.

That wasn't what mom bear wanted at all. I believe that the humans she'd seen were either super aggressive or running scared. She moaned loudly and stomped the ground, all the while keeping some bushes between us. I think my calmness upset her.

To soothe her, I stood up again and started talking to her in a calm voice. A couple of tracking friends were nearby on the next road and I called them on the radio. I wanted them to get a chance to see the bears so I stayed put, talking to the mother while they made their way to my spot.

As they walked up behind me, the mother bear had changed the sounds she was making. As my friends came close, they wondered who I was talking to because she had started to sound more human. She stopped pacing and was looking at me less out of fear and more out of curiosity.

When Jane and Kimber had spied the bears and spent a few minutes admiring their climbing skills, I suggested we leave so as not to prolong the stressful encounter for the mother. We made our way out of there, and left the general area to give her and the cubs room to move and feel safe again.

In a week or so, we went back to the site to look at the tracks.

It was interesting to see the claw marks on the tree where the cubs slid down and the marks they made going up, the broken branches and smashed vegetation at the base of the tree. The mother had made a "stomp trail" in the ground, a place where she moved forward and back stomping her paw prints into the forest floor. I found it very interesting to put my bike in the same place it had been the day of the encounter, then bend down to her viewing height to see what she must have seen of me. My impression that she had been sort of charging and stomping in my direction was correct, but she never got close to me. She had a spot where she stopped every time. It was where she could see me, but I couldn't see her.

Every time I read a story of a bear encounter gone wrong I always wish I could go there and read the tracks on the ground. I'm a very calm bear observer because of my time in Alaska, and I didn't understand her actions until I saw the tracks.

What a person perceives, particularly if they are scared or upset, and what really happened, which can be quite different, can be read on the ground. Of course, in any animal encounter, the human is free to make up any story they want to cover for embarrassing responses as, for sure, no one is going to be able to interview the animal.

Once I heard about a black bear attack on a man who was hunting. He was hospitalized for cuts and deep scrapes. His story that the bear came out of nowhere and attacked him was a little hard to believe, considering the nature of the black bears in Washington state. Later, a friend told me that the guy was pretty embarrassed that he had seen a bear and was running from it when he fell into a ditch full of barbed wire. The first story he told, the attacking bear, was so much more macho.

In reality, the bear was probably running the other direction just as fast.

The way you move in the wild is a cause-and-effect in your wildlife encounters. Because I have learned to see animal sign literally everywhere I look, I amble around in a rhythm given to me by nature. I walk about ten steps and pause, look around, up, and down, and then move on. When I do this, the birds keep making their companion and feeding calls, and the sound and feeling of the area around me goes on as if I am not there. When I hear the squirrels in the trees I passed ten minutes before go into alarm mode, I can tell there is someone on the trail behind me. Deer feeding in the meadow aren't alarmed by the human steps if the human is maintaining an ambling pace. Bears will become curious and possibly show themselves if a human sits quietly reading, sketching, or eating. Moving in wild time gives animals time to notice you, avoid you, and go on their way without having to interrupt their lives too much.

~ Mountain Lions ~

Many people also fear mountain lions. But they're a really hard animal to see. Many more mountain lions will see you than you see in a lifetime.

I have grown to love these big cats. They are so cat-like. They sleep like house cats, they slink like house cats, they would probably crawl into a big box if you left one in the road.

They also lead interesting lives where they actually develop a community and families. They use the landscape in a way that benefits, not only other animals, but the trees and plants as well. Bears dig up places and plant seeds for wild berries and other important food sources, and big cats feed the populations of other animals who need protein. A recent Panthera study noted that mountain lions interact with about five hundred species in their area. They are too important to habitat health to get rid of, simply because uninformed people are scared of them.

My strategy for staying safe around mountain lions sort of backfired for me. After seeing a couple big cats while I was alone in the wild, I decided that if one jumped on me, I would live. Working in the humane society as a volunteer, I learned that there is a spot in cats' mouths where you can grab their jaw and they can't bite you. It is on the lower jaw between their canine teeth. I also heard that big cats have delicate necks so I decided if a cat attacked me, I would grab it by the jaw and twist its neck. This violent thought seemed to cloak me in a different color to wild cats. I haven't been able to see one since. I miss my encounters with them.

But what should you do if you see one?

First, lucky you! Because these elusive cats are amazing to see.

Second, here's where you want to be tall, and show your personal power. You want to move with confidence and look at the cat. If the cat wants to investigate you closer, and you don't want it to, take a step towards it with the intention of scaring the shit out of it. It works to do that. I swear, the phrase "scaredy cat" must have come from cougars. In my experience, the three or four times I have had close encounters with them in the wild, they were really scared.

Once I was riding my e-bike midmorning on a back road on a loop ride. I came around the corner and spotted an animal in the middle of the road, headed in my direction. I thought it was a deer at first but then I saw the long tail and cat face.

I had stopped my bike and then as recognition came to me, I said, "Cool," jumped on my bike, and rode towards it to get a better look.

The look I got was the big cat sailing off the road and landing about fifty feet down the hill, running all-out.

Another time I was in my car, headed up a little-traveled, winding road when a cougar crossed in front of me. These were early tracking days for me so I immediately stopped the car and got out to look for tracks. I found them going up the steep bank on one side and pulled out my camera to document my find.

As I moved up the bank, though, I looked up and saw a bush shaking. I checked to see if there was a breeze and there wasn't. I looked hard at the bush until I could make out the legs of the lion. One of the back legs was nervously pumping up and down like a sewing machine. The cat was scared. I backed off a little and got to watch it bound out and over the overhang of the cliff above.

Another memorable time, my husband Mike was with me and we were riding up a paved, seven-mile hill when we came upon a dead deer. We got off the bikes to see it and it appeared very freshly killed.

The carcass had barely been opened. It looked like a cougar kill, with the stomach fur scraped off by teeth and the cavity just opened.

I suggested to Mike that we continue up the hill a ways and then, after a while, coast down silently to see if we could see the cat. When we came back, we just caught a glimpse of the animal dragging the deer off the road into the steep down side of thick vegetation.

~ Coyotes and Other Animals ~

If it's not lions, tigers, or bears then it's coyotes, owls, foxes, skunks, and even raccoons that people fear. In each case the fear is a lack of understanding or a belief in "facts" that just aren't true.

Coyotes are probably the most misunderstood animals we live with. They form strong family groups, and if left to their own devices, will not multiply past what the habitat can handle. In each pack, only two coyotes can mate. However, when humans disrupt the pack structure through hunting or "management," then the teenage coyotes can do as they please and coyotes multiply. Coyotes eat things like mice, rats. and ground animals that breed ticks. I never have understood why humans are afraid of them. I'm more afraid they will be wiped out and then we will have to deal with an over abundance of animals who carry disease to humans. It's the little things, like viruses and disease-carrying insects, that we should be afraid of. If we disrupt a working habitat, the resulting chaos can be downright dangerous.

The worst animal attack I experienced in the years I have been in the woods was from an animal the size of a golf ball. It was a wintry day and I had set off to find a little river through the deep woods. When I got to the banks, I looked for a place among the fallen trees to rest. I sat on a large downed limb with a view of the creek. But not for long, for out from under the tree came a little brown rocket of energy, screaming and pecking away at my jacket. I later learned it was a winter wren (now called Pacific Wren) and that I probably sat next to her nest. She chased me down the trail a ways for sure.

So any animal that you corner, cut off from their babies, or accidentally ruin their feeding site can get good and angry. They might even attack.

One good way to assure your safety in the woods is to move in a way to enhance, not diminish your awareness of your surroundings. Being safe around animals starts with you realizing that you are in their living room. They can't go to the store for food, so their life is centered around surviving; finding food sources, shelter, and water. They all have predators and must be wary, as they can't go to the hospital with injuries, either.

I'm often asked why I don't carry a gun. The short answer is that they are too heavy and in order for a gun to keep you safe, you need to know a lot about it and have practiced with it more than just a little. A gun is a big responsibility, as well. If you kill something, there may be legal consequences. If you are a savvy gun handler, understand the game laws and the enormity of killing a being by design or by accident, then a gun may make sense for you.

If not, consider carrying bear-sized pepper spray. Just carrying pepper spray changes the way you move. But like a gun, you need to know how to use it like any other tool. You also need to plan ahead. In a dangerous encounter with an animal, you may only have a few seconds to make a decision. Where is your pepper spray? It should be very handy. Mine lives in a side pocket of my front pack on my bike and I could, if need be, shoot it without getting off my bike. People I have encountered in the wilderness seem to notice the pepper spray and its proximity to my fingers. A couple of them have backed up while we were talking.

At Treesong Nature Awareness and Retreat Center one day

while teaching a beginners' tracking class, I had several cans of expired pepper spray on hand that were still good, but not safe to rely on. I decided to let the class experiment with the stuff.

I showed them how the safety works, and let off an orange stream into the bushes. The wind changed just as one student decided to walk over to me and it covered her with spray. She got a full dose of it and began sputtering and coughing. She ended on her knees on the ground. I felt really bad about that, but since I had had that experience myself a couple of times, I knew that just leaving her be for a few minutes was the best we could do. Then, when the effect starts to wear off, washing off the skin with white vinegar is the best way to treat it.

It's also important that you understand the effects of leaving it in your car in the sun. On a 90-degree day, it got to be 165 degrees in my car and exploded a can of pepper spray. A few hours later when I opened the door, the effects were still in full swing because of the heat. That's when I learned about the vinegar. I called the company who made the spray and after telling them the incident was all my fault, I asked them what to do. They said water will make it worse by spreading the oil around. The effects do wear off; it takes forty minutes or so before it fully dissipates.

Once you have experienced pepper spray, it is easier the second time. Really.

The first cool thing about pepper spray is that when you have it, you never seem to need it. Having it handy and knowing how to use it gives you confidence and makes you move differently. You no longer walk telegraphing fear.

The second cool thing is that if you have to use it on a person or an animal, the creature won't die. I suppose someone could sue you for using pepper spray on them, but even if they were successful, it wouldn't be nearly as bad as if you had shot them with a gun. I expect they also might have a hard time trying to explain away what they did to you to make you spray them in the first place.

With a little planning, knowledge, and care, you can make yourself feel safe around animals. Unless your job is to tackle them and tag them, you will communicate your intentions and your appreciation once you get over your fears.

Animal encounters are a wonderful thing to the backcountry traveler, and with a little understanding and empathy for the animal's life, each encounter can be a treasured gift.

~ 10 ~

Tracking by Bicycle

It seems a long way from being on your knees in the grass, looking at small smashed vegetation, to tracking from a bicycle. However, that transition is not so farfetched. One of the things you'll discover about tracking is that it takes all of your senses and the ability to change focus. It's also the ability to divide your focus.

When I'm standing in a group of people anywhere outside, part of my focus remains on the insects, birds, smells, and weather as I talk. This is a habit I developed while being alone in the wild, and it stays with me wherever I am.

My tracking friend Jane has developed this propensity as well. We can be talking to someone and suddenly we'll look at each other. We almost don't have to ask, "Do you smell that?" We might both have caught the faint aroma of carrion, skunk cabbage, elk smell, or the wet dog smell of a bear. All of them mean tracking opportunities. Smell is one of the senses that makes bike tracking feasible.

When you use your bike for a tracking tool, you ride differently. Your motive is not mainly exercise or learning more technical trail skills to go faster. Instead, you use your biking skills go slower, silently and efficiently.

Tracking by bicycle gets you to places where there are fewer humans. You can go a mile or two further, or approach wildlife-rich areas behind closed gates. It can allow you to move between habitats faster than going off trail. It also can give you miles of dusty or muddy track trap. By track trap, I mean an area where tracks show in the substrate. A dusty or muddy back road, not driven very often, can yield some interesting tracks and is certainly a good place to pick up the trail of an animal crossing. Animals who live in the area use the road for fast travel, or at least cross it, during their daily lives.

We've discovered, by keeping logs and image journals of our discoveries, that certain animals use different locations based on the season. We visit the areas that green up first in the spring, where the plants have more nutrition when they are newly growing and many animals feed on this bounty. You can learn to smell these areas from your bike as you ride through, just like you can smell ripe berries later in the year.

Fresh scat in the road, which is a favorite place for animals to advertise their presence and hunting abilities, offers a good place to stop. You know that an animal had to have paws on the ground in that spot to leave the scat, so it's time to get off the bike and change your focus to discover the small details. See if you can see the tracks or the little signs, like pebbles moved, to determine whether the animal was following the road or if it came up on the road to leave its odiferous "email." And, where did it go? Some great trailing opportunities come up from this kind of sign.

One ride we took a few springs ago gave us a great insight into a bear's day. There were three of us riding a little-used back road and Jane and I were stopping for all the fresh scats.

Our companion was a little confused about why we stopped for some of them and not others. That day, there had been a butterfly hatch and every fresh scat had telltale butterflies on it. The other ones were older and dried out; hence, they wouldn't yield as much information.

One such scat had a fresh companion next to it. It was a mother bear with cub and both left a calling card. The mother bear's scat was so fresh, it was still surrounded by a circle of urine that hadn't dried in the sun. We could tell that they came onto the road from a well-used but steep, multi-use trail. The scats were full of sedges and fresh spring green-up. They had come onto the road at an angle, left the scat, wandered the road a bit, then took off down into a very steep valley on the other side. Our bike route would be taking us to the bottom of the canyon later in the day.

Sometimes, you can be riding along, at a slow steady pace between seven and ten miles per hour, and you aren't seeing anything. If that happens, I stop anyway and look down the road I just came on. The light can be such that you don't see animal sign at all until you turn around and ride the road the other way. If you're planning a loop ride, take into consideration the location of the sun for the time of day you will be there. It's really hard to see sign and tracks if the light is wrong. Before you ride, make a track and move around it to see which direction highlights the shadows more clearly. It's possible to completely miss a line of sign if there are no shadows.

When I'm riding alone, I often plan an out-and-back ride so that I can track one side of the road on the way out and the other side on the way back. On more than one occasion, however, I've found new bear tracks on the way back.

One occasion that comes to mind is the day I was photographing rough-skinned newts in a puddle next to a back road. I left and explored down the trail for a couple of hours. When I rode back, I glanced in the puddle to see how the newts were doing. The puddle was muddy and settling as I watched. There was no evidence a car had muddied the puddle, so I got off the bike to look closer. The newts were mostly gone, but there were perfect fresh bear tracks in the puddle, under the water. Rough-skinned newts, by the way, are poisonous.

I watched for a while but couldn't tell if the bear made a mistake and ate the newts or whether it found the eggs to eat. This is one of the tracking mysteries I'm still working on. Every spring the newts come out of the river into the puddles to breed. When a car drives through the puddle it looks like they go underground. However, the bear that was in the area that spring tried to eat some poisonous fungus as well, and left big piles of unhealthy-looking scat the same color and texture as the fungus. Perhaps it was an orphan whose mother wasn't around long enough to teach it what not to eat. I'm pretty sure the bear lived and learned.

I find that unlike walking, a bike tire doesn't disturb the tracks in the road as much, as the bike tire can easily be discerned by its pattern and narrow but unbroken character. Walkers have a tendency to walk side by side, but trackers on bikes seem to be able to maintain a single file line of travel.

The more you ride and track, the less likely it is that you will miss something. It's hard to describe, but in covering more territory and returning to it often over the summer, you get a real feel for the natural events that happen in a location. I guess it's sort of like you have a bigger living room and when someone moves something or ruffles the pillows, you notice it.

Using tracking awareness skills while you're riding can help you survive as well. I scan the trail ahead while I ride, looking for track and sign automatically. I was on a remote back road once when I noticed a sparkle in the light on the trail ahead. When I got close, I stopped to see if I could find it. I did.

It was a taut fishing line, about eight inches from the ground, stretched across the trail. I put my bike down and carefully looked to see where it was coming from. I followed the line into the woods, stopping to look around every few steps. It was a good thing too, as I came upon a compound bow loaded by tension, and set to release if something tripped over the fishing line. I suppose I should have triggered it, but instead I pulled a log across the road. I put an X on the ground with flagging tape and made my way around the trap. When I was clear, I rode to the main road as quickly as I could, seeking cell service. I ran into a guy on a motorbike and told him about the trap. He rode off to call the sheriff's office. I don't see things like this very often, thank goodness, but I thank my lucky stars that anything out of place makes me stop.

One of my tracking friends calls me a "forest sign" tracker. I guess he means that I work on the signs of animal passage, such as browsing, scent marking, using multi-use trails, leaving scat, beds, and lay marks more than clear sign, like a paw print in mud. The habitat of the Pacific Northwest woods is a great place for a forest sign tracker.

Things change, though. Riding back roads is an adventure, even if you revisit the same areas. I try to check on the places I have tracked before, as well as add new areas every season. One of the trends I have noticed in doing this is that the forest service and the logging industry can completely change a habitat in a few days. If there is a timber sale, or a road needs to be cleaned for fire access, the big machines come out and scrape the road and trim the shoulders of encroaching vegetation.

Looking at these changes from an animal point of view, the routes that they took before and the crossings they used no longer carry their scent. Their carefully constructed routes marked by tracks and scent are wiped clean. Their scat is gone and the trail entrances are obliterated. The road no longer feels familiar or safe. They might be cut off from their feeding area, or the safe place they bedded down. Their patterns change for survival. For the bike tracker, it means that everything you knew about that habitat is now different.

Two summers later, when the road starts to take on a more organic feel again, little paws venture out onto the scary place and different animals use the road. The deer browse the new plants that come up as a result of new areas of runoff and the road starts to be shaded again.

Here is the conundrum. If someone didn't clean the roads once in a while, we couldn't even ride bikes on them.

Last summer I met a man who had a contract to clean roads. For part of the summer, it seemed I would run into his work area almost every other day. I finally caught up to him and we had a nice chat about roads. He and his partner were concerned about habitat. They seemed thoughtful in the way that they groomed the roads. When they were done, the animals were still using those roads, proving that it's possible to be gentler on the habitat than most big yellow machines are.

~ 11 ~

Kayaking and Tracking in Snow

Animals aren't used to people in boats. For some reason a person in a kayak, drifting close to shore quietly, doesn't seem to pose much of a threat to a wild animal. To a point anyway. That point seems to be when they make eye contact with you, or you raise a camera at them.

I got to watch a beaver at a small lake noisily grooming on a mud bank. I stayed motionless in my boat, drifting closer to the animal, pretty much just holding my breath. When we made eye contact, the beaver flipped around and slipped into the water. It was quiet for around three seconds and then wham! The tail slap hit right next to my boat, close enough to splash me. I chuckled and picked up my paddle to move back out into the lake. That beaver, though, wasn't done with me. I got schooled by several tail slaps and ushered away by a pretty mad-looking beaver.

Another time, another lake, I came upon a doe and fawn at the lake's edge for a drink. The mother looked at me intently but didn't deem me a threat. I stopped paddling to watch. They took their time drinking and then ambled away. I guess people in small boats don't usually shoot or chase deer.

Otters, especially young ones, don't seem to mind a quiet

kayak either. A friend and I got to watch some young ones at the edge of a river. We had noticed a little rock cave at the edge of the water where young otters popped in and out of the shelter. One young otter came out to sit on the shelf and interact with us. It had a shinny pebble with it and showed it to us several times. It reminded us of a little girl showing off her doll.

I've had ducklings try to hitch a ride and dragonflies use my deck for sunbathing. Fish seem to use me for shade if I am just drifting, while wading birds ignore me. But, I do a different kind of boating than most people. I call it swamp boating.

~ Swamp Boating ~

Launching in lakes or quiet parts of a river, I use my boat to go places I couldn't walk to, like into swampy, shallow, inlets where the animals hang out. I've discovered that if you have a stable recreational kayak, the kind with a skirt, you can put on a poncho, rain hat, and then the skirt. When you seal yourself in the boat you are pretty impervious to rain. Boating like that in the rain can be a really fun time, as you stay dry and comfortable. Especially if you have a thermos, some snacks, binoculars, and the time to take it easy.

So wildlife watching from a kayak is easy.

However, tracking from a kayak is not. If you are at water level, you can only see the tracks that are on the bottom of the lake. To see the ones on shore, you need to get out of the boat. That said, my kayak has been the means to get to some great tracking areas where dogs and people tracks are rare.

Some of my best plaster casts of tracks came from backwater, sandy areas that you couldn't get to any other way. Animals come to drink at places they feel safe and a tracker can find these spots from the water by looking at the shore vegetation. Low down at the bank you may see tunnels in the vegetation where animals move to and from the water regularly. When you find them, it's a good place to get out and look at tracks, follow the trail, and learn who lives there.

Messing about in boats has been a part of my life since I was a little kid. Currently you'll find more and more ways to get on the water. Your imagination offers the key ingredient to any boat you can afford. Any kind of boat—SUP (stand up paddleboard), inflatable, sit on top, canoe, or even a log raft—can supply fun if you think about where you can best use it.

Safety while boating is essential, and many others have supplied excellent references on this subject. But consider these elements:

If you can't swim, or are uncomfortable in the water, by all means go to a pool first and take swimming lessons.

Know the water you are in. Are there currents, winds, or tides to keep track of, and what's downstream?

Is it deep, shallow, or filled with rock?

What temperature is the water likely to be?

Plan your return as carefully as your entry into the water.

And so on. Common sense, and entering the watery world at your own pace, are key.

~ Snow Tracking ~

In winter, when the boats and bikes are all in the garage, it's time for snow tracking. Every year when the snows fall, people who have never seen tracks before start to notice them.

The classic scenario that happens online every year is the squirrel who bounds across a snowy deck somewhere. The person in the house looks out and sees "really big tracks" across their deck, right under their window, for heaven's sake! They are sure that a mountain lion looked in their window at them while they were watching TV. To the untrained eye, the four small feet of a squirrel in snow can make what looks like one track with four digits, as big as a mountain lion.

Snow tracking can be difficult, actually. It seems like it would be easy, and sometimes it is, but most times you are looking at a substrate that registers all too easily. Not only does every little thing register, like a stick blowing down your driveway, but the marks that things make in snow start to change as soon as they are born.

Some animals walk on the top of snow and others plow through. Some make deep trails that they use many times. Powdery snow can wipe out the passage of a huge animal like a buffalo in a short time, and some wet snow can keep the tracks of a vole for months.

Nonetheless, by going out tracking in snow you will learn a whole lot. And, you can use the same place over and over because as the fast weather changes, everything you saw just the day before can be gone, while a whole new story shows up there to be read.

Photographing or taking casts of tracks in snow can offer

a challenge, too. It is possible to use a waxy agent to prepare a perfect snow track for plaster. It takes a bit of practice, though, so pick a line of sign where there's more than one good track. Photographing snow tracks takes some awareness of your camera and fast-changing light.

I once found a trail of a mother mountain lion and her two cubs that stretched all the way down the road I was snowshoeing on. They were perfect in some spots as the cat didn't sink in the crusty snow, but the tracks were inset enough to be visible. It was nighttime and I wanted badly to get some photographs. I tried to set up my LED flashlight in a way that would cast the right shadows. I futzed around for quite a while. I'm sure if the cat was still in the area, it was pretty curious about what I could possibly be doing.

Finally, I hit on a solution. I dug a tunnel under a beautiful set of double register tracks and inserted the LED flashlight under the snow and under the track. The result was a pretty cool backlit image of the track that showed the details.

In spring, when the snow is soft and filled with tree debris, it might be hard to pick out fresh tracks if you don't realize that they will be the clean spots. Likewise, there may come a day when it looks like there are tracks all over the place, everywhere you look—until you notice that big plops of snow are falling out of the trees and marking up the landscape with craters that have no pattern.

What you learn in the snow can help you all year round. The tracks of a snowshoe hare can be pretty big, for example. In summer you may be looking at some odd-shaped tracks in the grass, thinking they are cougar tracks or something equally large, when you remember the snowshoe hare. Looking a little deeper, you might find the evidence of the rabbit gait (front paws landing and hind paws passing them up to land in front).

You can also store away in your memory bank which logs a marten loves to run up and down, and where animals tend to cross the creeks. Winter is a great time to look under bridges. Many animals take shelter there and leave tracks in the exposed dust or mud, where in summertime you might only find signs of domestic dogs and kids playing in the creek.

The important part is that you go out to look, no matter the weather. Trackers call it dirt time. What they mean by that is the time you spend out looking at tracks in the dirt, snow, mud, dust, grass, pine needles; in puddles, on fences, in vegetation and moss. Every time you go out, you can learn something new. The experiences you have doing so can't be replaced by any other study. Many things you learn in life can be done in a classroom, on TV, or in books, but tracking takes all that and dirt time. There is no substitute for your personal exposure to tracks in the wild.

~12~
Storytelling

No one forgets a story. Oral storytelling is an art. It's also a very human reaction to life. It's a way of sharing, learning, teaching, and relaxing.

Even sad and tragic stories have staying power, to be told again and again. Stories that make you feel good at the end, or want to go do something, change something, or experience something again, not only please you but anyone you share them with. Hopefully, your childhood was filled with stories which are part of your life.

Tracking and being outdoors are a breeding ground for good stories because nature is full of adventure, mystery, and surprises. Indigenous cultures around the world use the verbal story as a way to preserve their culture, educate their young, and learn more about their world—and so should the rest of us. It doesn't matter if it's on social media or in person, a good story sticks with you long after you hear it.

One of my favorite tracking stories happened while I was learning to track in snow:

~ Mystery Divots ~

I spent the day cross-country skiing and marveling over the clarity of tracks in snow, like the marks of the feathers as a bird took off. Some tracks were filled with details I hadn't seen before, and others were just a line of indistinct holes in the snow.

Sometimes, knowing what I was looking at took a while. I found myself trying to read the stories of animals while I was making my own story. My own tracks showed where I looked at squirrel tracks or dug in the snow to see how big a tunnel was.

As I was skiing back to my car on the trail, I noticed that in front of me there were four holes in the snow. They looked like they had just been made, as the divots had powdery snow debris around them, so I looked inside them to see if I could see tracks. They were deep. I tried to figure out how they got there, and if they even *were* tracks. I took off my skis so I could look at them carefully. I got my flashlight out of my pack and looked down in them. Yes, they were tracks, but I couldn't figure out of what, and how come there were only four of them?

I was confounded. But, I was also determined not to go on until I figured it out. The snow was registering pretty well, so I expected to be able to see more tracks, as I figured an animal that stood there couldn't just beam up to space. I got down on my knees to try and see better into the bottom of the holes. I happened to glance to the side and that's when I noticed the exit tracks. They were lightly etched on top of the snow and so fresh that there wasn't any difference between the color of the tracks and the snow around them. They were the four-digit, slightly asymmetrical, no claws showing, round-looking bobcat tracks. Ah ha!

But—why did the cat only sink in at that one spot?

I looked all around the deep tracks, with my head almost on the ground. Finally, I looked up.

Above the trail I saw a wide, horizontal limb of a fur tree. In the snow drift on the branch, I could just see the body impression of a bobcat.

So!

The cat heard me coming and jumped down.

Its legs were long enough that it didn't leave a body mark.

I was looking at its landing spot!

Then it walked into the forest on top of the snow, delicately, leaving hard-to-see tracks.

This story comes back to me every time I see a mystery on the trail that can't be easily solved. It's a reminder to me to keep looking, keep thinking, and keep changing focus, from up close to farther away, as I investigate. And to look up!

One of my favorite human tracking instructors, Joel Hardin, is fond of saying, "What is not looked for, will not be found." His experiences as a life-long tracker have shown him that people don't think they can see things, so they just don't even look.

Once in his class, we were standing in a field of long grass blowing in the wind as we looked for sign. Somehow a strand of my hair blew in my eye and got under my contact lens. I swiped my face as the tears started to flow and the hair flicked out the lens and sent it flying. I don't remember what I said, but Joel, who was standing behind me, said not to move. Slowly and carefully, he moved forward and then bent down into the grass and gently picked up my lens and handed it back to me. Where my first thought was that I would never find it, his was to look for it.

~ An Uneasy Feeling ~

Looking for explanations and not ignoring the questions leads to discovering story after story.

For instance, a night out snowshoeing might turn into a full-on mystery to be solved, like the time I went to a ridge I had found and snowshoed to the end of it. In the last evening light I could see Mt. Hood with its pink, late-day glow. My plan was to spend some time watching night fall with a cup of hot chocolate before I snowshoed back to my car.

I stood there, however, and pictured myself doing that but somehow I was reluctant. I had an uneasy feeling.

As the tree shadows extended in my direction, the feeling grew stronger. I'd had fun looking at snowshoe hare tracks, bird tracks, and a few coyote tracks on the way in. The snow was deep but with a fluffy layer of new snow on top that showed tracks clearly. I looked around me and tried to feel comfortable but the reality was, I just didn't.

After a discussion with myself about the uneasy feeling, I allowed myself to head back to the car. I followed my own trail, putting my snowshoes in the trail I had already broken, which made for easier walking. As I went, I felt even more uncomfortable but I couldn't understand that feeling.

It wasn't until I got to my car, took off my snowshoes, and opened the back hatch that I felt a sigh of relief. It's just not like me to get scared. I shook my head in wonder at myself, but even as I chastised myself for being silly, a shiver ran down my spine, causing me to shudder.

I was starting to take off my snow clothes when I heard a siren. Well, not just one, but a whole fleet of ambulances, echoing through the canyons on the still, cold night. I stopped and looked around but I couldn't see anything; no lights, no shadows, nothing to give me a clue. Then the sounds changed and I realized I was listening to a pack of coyotes. They sounded alarmed though. Not the usual joyous howls, but as if they were scared too.

In a few minutes they stopped. I stood listening as it grew completely quiet.

It's a good thing I was at my car because I felt absolutely haunted. Not a night bird, the *swish* of a tree branch, or the crunch of a footfall. *Nothing.*

The next morning I got up and got dressed to go back there. I was packing my car when I got a call from a friend who said she wanted to go with me. I told her I was leaving in an hour. She said she could make it.

We drove up to the place I had parked and got out. It was a partly sunny, very cold day and we headed off on the trail I had broken. I showed her some of the tracks I saw the day before, and when we got part way out on the ridge, I stopped.

In front of me, as clear as a track in a trail guide, glistened a cougar track—right in the middle of my snowshoe track from the night before.

I went into full-on discovery mode, looking at every track in the clear line of sign, backtracking the cat to where I had been standing and hesitating to sit down to make a hot chocolate. The cat had been in the trees near me. When I turned and left the night before, it followed me, using the shadows of the trees and walking down them, then switching to another tree, until it finally came out onto my trail and was stepping in my steps. When I re-tracked the cat forward on my trail, I found a spot where it veered off as I got close to the car. The trail led to the cliff's edge.

That was when my friend looked at her watch and said she had to be back in Stevenson by five for a date. Of course had she told me that before we left, I would never have taken her. I couldn't understand how a date could take priority over following cougar tracks! Unfortunately, my investigation was cut short.

By the time I was able to get back to the ridge, almost all the snow was gone, but I remembered the dead stump at the point where the cougar had turned off. I made my way down to the edge of the cliff there and looked over.

About five feet down, I could see a wide shelf that went under an overhang. As I was looking at it, a hummingbird came up to my face and then darted into a small opening on the ridge. I looked where it went and was able to find a safe way to get down to the wide soft spot, where I found coyote scat and tracks in the cave created by the overhanging cliff.

I decided that the timing had been right for the cat to have dropped in on a pack of coyotes and caused the alarm I heard.

I also thought that if the cat had wanted to pounce on me, it sure could have, at any time during my trek back to my car. Instead, it was probably curious, as all cats are. I know if the tables were turned and I found its tracks first, I would have followed it too. More investigation revealed that at the far end of the ridge, where I had decided not to make hot chocolate, there was a well-used animal path up and down that led towards the river in the valley. Part way down there was another cave in the rocks. It was abandoned, at least I thought it was, but it looked like every other cougar or bobcat den I have ever seen.

Shortly after I was there that last time, the road was decommissioned and ripped up by someone who was way overzealous in using the big equipment. They left no way to even walk through the debris. Ironically, a timber sale this year required them to rebuild the road but it's closed while the trucks are going in and out. Perhaps someday I will be able to get back to that ridge again. Perhaps it holds even more story. It's on my list.

~ Addictive Fun ~

It's the mystery and the solving that are so addicting. Think about all the people who love to read mysteries and all the writers who think up ways to flummox them. Stories, mysteries, and human curiosity. They all are part of tracking.

One of the byproducts of watching television and movies is that the details of a story are given to you. The colors, what the characters look like, what the scenery is, and the whole setup leave little to your imagination. Even the body language of the characters shows you just what you are supposed to think about what happens.

On the other hand, if you read a book, or listen to someone telling a story, you must fill in the blanks and use your mind and imagination. It's an exercise that is overlooked as one that can keep you healthy. Imagination is another "muscle" that responds well to exercise.

The art of telling a good story, of course, is first to have one to tell. The second key is to tell the story in a way that is engaging and interesting. You can start with the ending, but only if the rest of the story is not predictable. It's best to keep the "ah ha" moment until the end, without hints.

A Native American storyteller I admire told a story about the dog people. It seems when the Creator was ready to make people, or "two-leggeds," he made a deal with the dog people that they could party and dance like the two-leggeds, but just for one night. So they all stood on their hind legs and took off their tails so they could dance the night away.

When the sky got rosy, they remembered that the Creator warned them that they must go back to being dogs before dawn. They scrambled to find their tails and present themselves as dogs to the Creator just as the sun rose. In the hurry to find tails, though, things got mixed up. That's why today when two dogs meet they sniff each other's butts, still looking for their rightful tail.

Cute story, but whenever Mike wants me to repeat it for somebody he says, "Tell the story about why dogs sniff each other's butts." Of course, I can't tell it then because it's not interesting if you know the punchline ahead of time. And I wrote you a condensed version. I would never be able to tell it the way I first heard it from a Native American storyteller. He had his audience sitting on the edge of their seats because when you tell a story in person, you can create a whole atmosphere with gestures, facial expressions, and the use of unexpected words, phrases, and suspense.

The same storyteller related how a woman, noticing his native dress, once asked him where he hunted. He looked at her with an inscrutable facial expression, with the serious and exotic demeanor of a warrior, and dead-panned, "At Safeway."

The trick is to use people's "consensus of knowledge" and twist it. I mean, we all know that Native Americans hunted for meat, don't we? There are lots of things that we all "know." That's why jokes are funny. We all "know," for instance, that mothers-in-law are a problem, blonds are ditzy, and men with fat bellies drink beer. Not in reality, but in "consensus knowledge."

A good story uses the "knowledge" we all share and uses the tale to open our minds to new ways of looking at things. Like we all know that bears are scary monsters and will jump out of the bushes and eat your face off. Except, they aren't.

When I was finished working in Alaska at the bear-viewing lodge, I'd become a person filled up with stories. I wrote *Lonesome for Bears: A Woman's Journey in the Tracks of the Wilderness* to share the antics of the bears we got to know there. Then, when the book was published, I started giving talks on bears at various venues.

What I discovered about talking in front of people is that if you are into your story, you soon forget all about yourself. Once you do that, you can pay attention to your audience. You notice the looks on faces, the yawns, if there are any, and it becomes apparent that you might be up there telling a story, but it takes an audience to shape the story as well. It's still a group exchange even if you are the only one talking.

The best storytellers have a good story, a funnybone, a sense of human emotion, and a way of talking that is their own. Talking with a microphone can ease up the impulse to talk loud, which is really hard to listen to. Talking with ease, and in a regular or more quiet tone, is restful and effective. If you're telling a story around the dinner table or the fire, be aware that projecting your voice can ruin your delivery. Have people come in closer.

If you're speaking in public, try to set yourself up for success by setting some guidelines. For instance, when I give talks on bears, I let thc audience know that I will be into my stories and that I will entertain questions at the end of my talk.

Just like social media, get used to the idea that anything you tell people can and will go far and wide. They will record you with their phones and borrow parts of your stories to tell friends. Just like I used the Native American stories above to illustrate a point, your stories will go public. If you're working on a book or research that is sensitive, don't share until it's time. Then, like letting a soap bubble go, send your story into the universe.

When I hear that my stories about bears, tracking, and wilderness adventures have taught something or enhanced someone else's journey, that makes it all worthwhile for me.

Even if it doesn't seem like it on the surface, humans are deeply involved with animals. Stories about tracking and animals are engrossing, and like drumbeats, they are compelling. Storytelling draws people.

Little Foot

~ 13 ~

Dog Friends

Speaking about the dog people, let's talk about going out with your dog. I do understand "dog guilt" and the desire to give your dog, who is stuck in a human world, a quality of life. Your dog loves to be out in the wild. And because I do too, I totally understand that.

Your dog will hit the trail tracking and looking for adventure. It is a glorious thing to see how happy they get with the smells of wild places. Many hikers and dogs who have been on the trails for years understand each other's signals, and also know which animals to leave alone.

Then there are *most* dogs, whose nature is part wild but their upbringing in civilization has in no way prepared them for the hard lessons of a wild life.

Knowing the difference in dog skills is part of creating a safe experience for both the human and dog pal. The wisdom to avoid trying to play with porcupines or chase a bear in fun doesn't come naturally to our canine friends.

I can't tell you how many times I have just been recording some fresh mountain lion tracks and come across a dog owner who is giving their dog a wild experience by letting the dog run at will, off leash. The owners of these dogs would have a heart attack if they knew that their furry friend was running around in an area where a cougar hunts. Dogs chase cougars and cougars hate them. Sometimes the cougar will tree or, if they can, they will get in a good swipe at the dog.

Statistically, bear maulings and scary bear encounters often include the presence of a domestic dog. Without specific training, an off-leash dog will attack a bear and then naturally run back to the owner for protection. Seeing your off-leash dog barreling your way on the trail with a pissed-off bear right behind can ruin your day. The usual body language and standing your ground defenses might not work on a bear who has just been bitten in the butt by a dog.

Porcupines move slowly but they have no qualms at all about brushing up against a dog with their quills.

And then there's the damage a dog can do, say, running off a herd of elk who needed the time to graze, or biting into the leg of a deer whose wound slowly festers.

Unfortunately, hiking with a dog can also limit your own experience. The dog can have a great day, seeing and detecting lots of wildlife, but the owner goes home thinking there was nothing there. A few times out with the dog can convince people that there isn't anything to worry about where they go. The animals in the area start hearing the bird alarms of a dog on the trail as soon as the dog gets out of the car. If dogs could talk, they would have some wild stories to tell, while the tame hike that the human experiences in their company is something else.

To other humans on the trail an off-leash dog is a threat. They run fast and come barreling in your direction while the owner yells out commands that are ignored by the dog and end with, "Don't worry. He's friendly." Which is kind of like saying your check is in the mail, or I'll call you. An empty sentiment. If the owner of the dog has no voice control over a loose dog, the owner also has no idea what the dog will do when it reaches you.

If you are in the wild and a loose dog comes at you, treat it like any other wild animal. Stand your ground and prepare for the worst. Prepare your pepper spray. The dog might hit you hard and dislocate a knee or jump up on you, or it might run behind you in preparation for biting heels or thigh. Dog bites can be serious medical problems, so take it seriously. On the other hand, don't make the mistake of thinking a dog you don't know will let you pet it. Don't stick out a "friendly" hand until you have established a relationship with a strange dog. A dog that is barking and wagging its tail should calm way down before you decide it's not a threat.

I was off the trail one day, photographing and measuring some animal sign, and an off-leash dog that I had heard in the distance came up to me. I watched it approach. reading its body language as it made its way into my personal space. First it sat down and looked at me with no threat implied, then smelled me. We agreed to a pat on the head before the dog ran back to the owners who were loudly coming up the trail. After touching base with them, the dog ran back to me and wanted to hang around, seeming to prefer my company. The owners started calling for him but he wouldn't budge. The dog was interested in what I was doing, as he sniffed the bear trail and looked to me to see if I was reacting. Sometimes I wonder if dogs run away on purpose. Is it possible that their life among humans is kinda like being in jail?

This particular dog seemed thoughtful, even in the swirl of fresh bear smells I was in, and he watched me intently. The owners kept calling in the distance. Finally, they headed back to the trailhead. I had to walk the dog out to them. They were shocked to see me, and quickly leashed the dog and shoved him in the truck. I can't remember the exact words, but I do remember that they eyed me suspiciously, as if I had tried to steal their dog or was some lunatic hanging about unseen in the forest.

My advice to dog owners is pay attention to your dog's education if you want it for a hiking companion. Make sure it knows not to play with snakes, play chase with wild animals, or kill rabbits for fun.

Best of all would be to keep your dog on a leash while it learns about the wilderness. Pay attention to the dog's body language. Explore with your dog. If he runs across an interesting smell, see if you can see what it is. Even on a leash, if the dog has an owner wanting to learn, the partners can use each other's skills to find out more about the wild.

If you run into other people on the trail, check how your dog reacts to them. Unless you're a tracker, it's easy to get caught thinking no one else is going to be there and leave your dog off leash.

However, if your leashed dog has a strong reaction to other people, pay attention. Even a neophyte wilderness traveling dog has wisdom to share with the leash holder.

And as the leash holder, make sure you can actually hold it. I have been bumped hard by a dog whose owner was dragged part way down the trail as their dog overpowered them.

~ The Big Picture of Hiking with a Dog ~

Decide on the route that your dog can handle

Make sure you're prepared for the weather

Plan to take enough water and food for both you and the dog

You are your dog's protection, not the other way around.

A domestic dog hasn't got much say in the way their lives go. If you want a longtime faithful companion, it's a lot of work. You have to pay attention to the details, like what the substrate might feel like with bare paws, how hot it is, or cold, and how your dog's health dictates how far they can comfortably travel.

It's also important to pick up your dog's poop, even in a wild spot. Our wild animals can pick up a plethora of diseases from domestic animals. Since we have wiped out fifty percent of the wild animals on earth in the last two hundred years, we should all do our part to keep the ones we have left safe.

I don't have a dog, although there are quite a few dogs that I love. My desire is to have the experience of learning what the wild animals are doing and how. I want to be the explorer on the front line, using all my senses and attention for that purpose. The responsibility and work a dog requires would definitely cut into my tracking time.

Because I love animals, many have asked me *why* I don't have a dog and my answer is that all my pets are wild. That doesn't mean I pet wild animals, feed them, or manipulate them so I can see them. It means I appreciate their lives as they live them.

And it can be just as heartbreaking to lose a wild pet as a tame one. The male cougar I tracked for ten years went missing two years ago. I still look at his neglected scent-marking spots every time I go by them. I miss his tracks, the female cats with whom he shared territory, and the excitement of being in his presence. The animals he used to feed as a byproduct of his kills have disbursed as well. The habitat where he roamed seems forlorn, waiting for another majestic cat to fill his place. If he was harvested by a human hunter, I hope they get as much joy out of his dusty, mounted body as I did out of his very alive one.

~ 14 ~

Lost

There's an art to getting lost. For some of us it comes naturally and for others it takes some doing. All of us, though, can get lost.

Personally, I love route finding and looking at maps. Plus I was a boat captain for a while and had to learn navigation back when we didn't have GPS to help. So for me, getting lost is a challenge.

The first time I got truly lost, I was on a solo bike ride in an area I hadn't visited before. I had a map and compass in my pack, where most people keep them, but I took a wrong turn by making an assumption that the most traveled route was the one I wanted. Unfortunately, I didn't realize my mistake until I was a few miles into it. What made me realize that I wasn't at all where I expected to be was when I came up on a rise and saw Mt. Hood, one of the Oregon/Washington Cascade volcanos, right in front of me. It was the wrong mountain.

I should have been looking at Mt. Adams.

It was also getting dark and I didn't have any lights, as I expected to only stay out for the afternoon. (This ride was part of my learning experience early on.) As they say in search and rescue, "Expect the unexpected."

Panic set in. Then disbelief. That voice in your head that tries to mess you up told me to just keep going; it will sort itself out. Fortunately, I realized my car was to the north and Mt. Hood was to the south, so I shouldn't be headed that way.

I must say, there seems to be a part of human nature that doesn't want to turn around. Part of you argues, "But I still want to see what's up ahead!" And it's not only men who are reluctant to ask for direction, or look at the map again. I finally convinced myself to turn around.

Riding back, I noticed that Mt. Adams was obscured by clouds, and that the turn I was supposed to make was not marked because the sign lay in the ditch. There were cattle standing around at the intersection. They were actually blocking the road and looking at me. Looking at me in a mean, curious way, sort of like the bullies at school who are just waiting to see if you're going to do something dumb so they can thump on you.

I did a bait-and-switch. I made them think I was going to push my bike up the little hill on the side of the road and go around them. They moved, in their cow way, towards me. When the last one put its hooves in the grass I jumped back on my bike and rode down the hill to the center of the road faster than they expected.

I made it back to my car just as the last light faded. As I put my bike in the car, the stars came out. I looked up wondering which was my lucky one.

Route finding is fun and it takes you on some great adventures, but it does require some basic skills. Even if you always go with other people, you need to know these skills and practice them often.

~ Route Finding Skills ~

Basic directions, such as which way the ocean lies from where you are, should always be in your mind. It's a mistake to trust that someone else is thinking about these things for you. And stuff happens, like signs get knocked down or it gets dark.

"It's easy, you can't miss it."

"Don't worry, I know a shortcut."

These are only two of the comical things said too often in all seriousness. You owe yourself your own map.

Having a compass really helps, even if members of your group have fancy GPS units.

Lots of times, you only need to know the four points of the compass from where you are standing to figure out where you are on the map. It's possible that you have a compass app on the phone in your pocket, and you might not even realize it.

An example would be, say, that you and two others are on a bike ride. You come to an intersection where there are three choices besides turning back. You are trying to complete a loop and your friend pulls out the GPS to decide which road to take. Most of the time that works, but sometimes the GPS doesn't have a good signal, is out of battery power, or it has the wrong information. It wouldn't hurt to pull out your map and compass to back up the information given by the GPS.

You can find north on the compass by holding it flat, away from the metal of your bikes. You might consider things like deviation and declination but to start, the general direction of north is more important than fine tuning. The red needle will search for north so turn the compass until the north arrow on the compass rose matches the needle. That direction is generally north. Cool. Then take your map, and *unless it says otherwise,* the top of the map will always be north. Put your map down so the top of it matches the direction north on your compass.

By checking the direction of all the roads at the intersection, you can see which intersection is your location on the map. Say one of the roads you see goes west, one comes in from the southeast, and another goes north. Look on the map in the area you think you are and see which intersection matches those directions. Guess what! That's exactly where you are.

Knowing exactly where you are and using the map, you can easily see where you need to go. And if that matches the information on the GPS, you are good to go. If it doesn't, I would trust the map. I have seen too many times where the GPS certainly might have the coordinates of where you are but the translation into where you should go from there is lost in the fact that the maps the GPS program used were old, out of date, or simply not accurate.

Just yesterday a couple on a sketchy, cliff-hanging, slide-prone, single-lane road stopped me to ask where a certain campground was. Their GPS had sent them to the hill the campground was named after, instead of the camp. They were good and lost.

But what if you aren't on roads?

Again, find north on the compass and then put your map down under it to match the direction. There are ways to find out exactly where you are by taking bearings off visual points you can see and making an X on the map where they cross. But rather than lose you here with long explanations and instructions, let me share with you a trick that works every time. At least, it's worked for me every time.

On the map, locate the general area you are in. Then look for features on the map that go a long way in one direction, like a road that goes east and west, or a river that goes north and south. You should, by relaxing and taking a good look at the map, perhaps over a cup of tea (we will get to that later), be able to identify the area you are in. The realization that there's a road to the north of you that goes east and west is your salvation. Even better if you recognize that it's also the road you parked on.

Here's the trick: Pack up your tea break things and get ready to walk. With just your compass, sight it in on a tree or feature that you can easily see that is north of you. Walk to that tree or feature. Then do it again, holding the compass in front of you, sight in on something that you can see that is north of you. You will hit the road, because if you keep going north, it is a huge long object that you can't get around. Once you come to the road, you may recognize it, or you can use the map to tell which way to go.

Years after I got lost the first time, and after being in search and rescue for a few years where we studied a thing called "lost person behavior," I was out by myself snowshoeing in a blizzard. I was purposely trying to get lost because I wanted to see if what they taught us was true.

It was. When I was good and turned around from following snowshoe hare tracks, it was also getting dark and harder to see. I decided to head back to my car. I stopped and looked around and determined that my car must be off to my left. I was sure of it.

Then I took out my GPS and let it get some satellite data. The GPS said my car was off to the right of me.

"Geez, I knew that thing was a piece of shit!" I exclaimed out loud.

So I took out my map and compass to prove that the GPS was delusional. The map and compass showed the same thing.

And this shows you how badly a lost person can reason.

I thought, I seriously thought, there was something wrong with my compass. Anger flushed my face and I almost let myself stomp off to the left toward my car, which was my false sense of where I was. Had I done as all my instincts suggested, it would have put me at the edge of a very unstable and slippery cliff.

My voice of reason prevailed over the emotional voice and I used the compass to head north to a tree I could see, which was on my right at the time. A few tree sightings to the north and I came right out on the big parking lot where my car sat.

You need to know this:

A perfectly normal, sane person can become unreasonable in a situation where they are lost.

You may be out with a person who lets the emotional voice rule. And you might need to use diplomacy and tact to keep everyone safe.

Another time, actually the only other time I have been lost, I had been following a bull elk who was a wily old coot and led me on a very convoluted trail. When I gave up trying to catch up to him, I realized I had no idea where I was in particular, but I knew I was south of the road my car was on.

This time, after having the experience of irrational lost person behavior, I made myself pull out my little propane stove and heat some water for tea. I found a perfect log to sit on, on my poncho, while I sipped tea and watched big snowflakes coat the trees. When I was rested, hydrated, and warm, I set off to find my car using the trick of sighting in on trees in the direction I wanted to go. Within thirty minutes I was headed home in my car with the heater on.

Try this. At least do the exercise of aligning the map with north on your compass. These simple ways of dealing with navigation should keep you safer, even if you are with a someone who seems like they know everything you don't.

The other advantage of having a paper map is avoiding hazards. The GPS gives you the same information as a map, but the little screen makes it hard to focus on things like rivers and drop-offs. A shortcut from waypoint to waypoint doesn't include things like rock falls, downed trees, and weather-related hazards. With a map you can look at the elevation lines, which give you an idea of the flat places and steep canyons and cliffs. That's why I encourage you to have your own map to look at, even if you are with a group.

I have started using my iPad for photographs and journaling and found that there are a few very useful navigation apps. *Trailforks* and *onXBackcountry* are two that I found very useful if you also use your compass app so you can orient yourself. I still carry a hard-copy map because there are some things, like being able to recognize distant peaks, that maps just do better.

The danger of relying on someone else to know where you are and where you should go is a real one. Faulty thinking in serious situations is not uncommon. If you can remember these simple navigation tools, you should be able to find the way. Many more people die every year from being lost than being killed by wild animals. Take it seriously.

~15 ~

Sh*t Hits the Fan

So, what if something really goes wrong? Something catastrophic that you can't prepare for? Like what if you're out riding your bike alone and when you try to ride back to your car, you discover a rock slide and a big section of the road has fallen down the mountain, leaving you blocked off.

Well, once again, I guess it's time to stop, make yourself comfortable, and wait for the answers to come to you.

Nature, as a whole, mainly moves about as fast as ice melts. Humans are used to a much faster pace that demands answers right away. When things get real, if we slow down to nature time we have a better chance to survive.

Of course, your first inclination might be to see if you could climb over the rocks and get by, or if you can push your bike up the hill and go above it. That is the surest way I can think of to make a bad situation potentially lethal.

While you're pausing, you may notice that slowly and underneath it all, the slide is still moving. If you listen, you might even hear it. As you consider your situation, you'll notice that you aren't in immediate danger. As a matter of fact, being cut off from the road you're quite safe, even from other people.

Then you will review where you are and what other ways

you could get back to your car. The map comes out. The compass comes out and a solid, thought-out plan comes to you. If there isn't any way, then you set up your camp to wait for help.

A slow response might have just saved your life.

In Lawrence Gonzales' book, *Deep Survival: Who Lives, Who Dies, and Why,* the author points out that in the middle of a catastrophic event, we have about six seconds in which we can manipulate the outcome. People who use those six seconds can often change an outcome, if only enough to survive.

I was riding down a steep, single-track trail with some friends when I looked at the next switchback and decided it wasn't within my capabilities to ride it. I got off my bike, which was a pack-loaded e-bike at the time, held onto my brakes and handlebars, and tried to maneuver the bike slowly down the slippery turn. It was so steep that my tires slipped out and the bike started sliding down the steep part on its side. I was still holding on and sliding with it when the toe of my boot caught on a root. Next I was airborne, and while I was in flight I had the thought that the one place I didn't want to land was on my bike.

Somehow, and I'm not sure how, in those few seconds I managed to fly out ahead of my bike and land on the trail.

Of course I got scraped up and my face hit the dirt, but I didn't break anything. I rolled over and managed to put a hand out to stop my bike from hitting me. Everything stopped. I sat up and assessed the damage, which was mostly scraped skin and dirt.

I sat on the trail for a few minutes and tried to figure out how I had managed to do that, as I clearly remembered my bike on its side and my body stretched out just above it. It was a mystery, but I all I can determmine is that my strong thought to miss the bike propelled me just a bit further.

Things do happen sometimes that you can't be prepared for. These things can happen in your house, too, so you shouldn't let them keep you indoors. What you can do is think of things that typically happen and attempt to prepare solutions. Like, when I think of big trees falling in the forest, I know there probably would be a big cracking sound and, if I ever hear it, I have studied downed trees and what things in the forest you can duck behind or under to keep from being squashed.

These imaginary situations are a training tool for yourself. When I am out alone, I try to observe potential dangers wherever I am. It's different from being scared and thinking negative thoughts, though. It should be commonsense things that are based on observation and not just imagination.

If you are out on a day that black clouds begin forming at the horizon, watch for distant lightning and the sound of thunder. Get yourself to an area of protection as soon as you can. Don't be macho. Recognize the danger and move.

"What's a matter? You scared of a little lightning?"

Hell yes, and why not? People get killed by lightning and there is no good reason to tempt fate. Take a clue from the animals that live there and make yourself safe from lightning, hail, and strong winds. If you are in the desert and there is a storm in the mountains, be wary of traveling in dry washes. Flash floods are just exactly that. They happen in a flash.

Reactive groups of humans can be like schools of fish. Someone makes a move and they all follow. Then the ones on the outside of the group get picked off by bigger fish. If you are in a group that chooses to ignore observable present danger, get away from them if you can't reason with them. After all, someone has to be okay in the end to call for help.

~ Survival vs. Prevention ~

There are lots of schools and books on survival techniques. It's really good to know how to start a fire in the wet snow or how to make a debris hut. Making animal traps and water stills are for long-term survival and those skills are handy to know about even if you never have to use them. But here's hoping you learn enough never to get in a survival situation in the first place.

Personally, I think learning survival skills is starting at the wrong end of the stick. If you end up lost or hurt in the wilderness with nothing, it will be because you already made a whole series of bad decisions.

As a member of a search and rescue group, I was once invited to take a class from a top Air Force survival teacher. I'm afraid I didn't do very well. When they told me we were supposed to leave our packs behind and spend the night on the hill above camp, I politely excused myself and went home. I could see what was going to happen and I didn't think I needed to do that to myself on purpose.

That said, I have studied the techniques and practiced them on my own. Part of what the military does to you is make you tired, cold, and hungry on purpose and then see if you can perform. Many hard lessons are learned in that. There is a point at which any human loses the ability to rationally think things out. The military instructors are very good at stretching that point and making tough people. Only it doesn't have much shelf life, and you have to keep doing it to stay that tough.

My philosophy is to avoid putting yourself in the situation where you have to "survive." Part of keeping with my way of being comfortable and peaceful in the wild is not to let others lead you astray. There is a place for the survival discipline, and some very good instructors, but that sure doesn't include a good and serene, fulfilling time in nature.

However, there could come a time when the unavoidable happens to you and knowing what to do will save your life. Part of it, believe it or not, is your ability to get dirty.

One of the interesting statistics about search and rescue operations is that little kids, under five or so, have a much greater chance of surviving a couple of nights alone in the wilderness than older ones. Part of the reason for that is they aren't afraid to get dirty.

~ Dirty, But Still Alive ~

If you're caught out unprepared, say it's getting cold and you don't have a warm enough jacket or shirt, stuffing your clothes with dry leaves will give you another layer. If you can't make a fire and it's raining and cold, crawling into a dry tree well, going so far as to dig out the dry dirt and cover yourself with it, can save your life. Just make sure that if you do that, you leave something colorful on the surface for searchers to find.

I once sprained my ankle up on a snowy road where I was hiking by myself. It was bad enough that I couldn't walk. I had a couple of choices.

First I made myself comfortable where I had landed and took a pain pill with some coffee from my thermos. The pain subsided a bit, and I decided to try and get to my car anyway.

I packed my boot with snow to take down the swelling and then crawled around until I found the right stick to make a cane. I ended up with two of them and I was able to hobble my way down to the car. Fortunately, even though it was my right ankle, I was able to drive my stick shift using my left foot for the clutch.

My other choice would have been to make camp, make myself as comfortable as possible, and wait for help.

Since I now take emergency supplies with me on every day outing, I would have been semi-comfortable. I had a poncho with which to make a shelter and the materials I needed to make a fire. But I calculated how long it would take for me to be reported as missing, for the search group to find me, and the trouble it would require to carry me out. It seemed like the pain of hobbling to my car, no matter how long it took, would be less.

The point here is that your best survival tool is being able to think clearly. That's why delaying immediate action is so important. Unless you are in the air falling, or in the middle of an avalanche or rock slide, stop first and calm yourself into a state where you can make rational and logical decisions.

If there are others with you, listen to their ideas and evaluate the action they propose. You don't have to take their word for it; think it out yourself. Even if you are being guided, guides can make mistakes. You can make the point that talking out a plan is more important than who is in charge. Ask questions.

For instance, "So if we take this trail down to the road on the other side of the hill and we reach the road…then what? Will one of us have the energy to walk to the cars or will we have a cell signal? Will that put us in a place where a rescue crew would never think to look for us? Have you been on that road before?"

It would be sad to have to say to yourself later, "If only I had just gone with my plan and not listened to the cockamamie idea they came up with."

Consensus makes teamwork. If everyone talks out a plan and they all agree, then everyone will put their energy into it. Even a good plan can be ruined by one person dragging down the energy through obstinance.

Also, be willing to stand your ground for yourself. I would split off from a group before I would do something I thought was stupid or counterproductive. If you're in a pickle and it's a work group you're with, going your own way can be sticky. Just remember, your life and well-being take priority over your job.

~ Your Job—or Your Life? ~

Once, I was running a yacht from San Francisco to San Diego with the owner and a friend on board. We stopped in Santa Barbara for an overnight rest. In the morning the generator wouldn't start. The owner wanted me to just leave anyway, saying it was a short run to San Diego and we could get along without the generator.

I disagreed. I wanted to find the problem and fix it before going out in the ocean again.

But my boss was the kind of guy who didn't like his employees telling him what to do. He insisted we leave.

I thought about it for a few minutes, then said, "Well, go ahead. I think I'll just take my bag and find the train station."

He sort of went into shock.

I packed.

Then, he wanted to talk about it.

I told him when one thing goes wrong, it's very likely to add up to other things going wrong. Without knowing why the generator quit, there was no way I was going to risk the boat and well-being of myself and their two lives just for convenience' sake.

And, as I pointed out to him, my Coast Guard license took me five years to get, whereas jobs were easier to find.

After about half an hour he said, "Okay, take the time to find out what's wrong."

I put my bag down and went down to the engine room to figure it out.

Turned out, the generator was out of fuel because the last time we had fueled up in Morro Bay, the owner told the dock hand not to fill the forward fuel tank. Of course I had previously asked him to fill it up. The dock boy decided to follow the owner's instructions instead of mine. I didn't know this. The owner didn't know that the generator only fed off the forward tank.

There are times when you need to look at the big picture and not just your job. Just like there are times when the big picture is more important than someone's feelings.

One lesson that surprises people who join search and rescue is that, in an emergency situation, you are to consider, first, yourself, then, your teammates, and last, the subject you are trying to help.

If you think about that, it isn't selfish; it's completely necessary. If you're not okay, you can't help anyone else.

~ 16 ~

That Cup of Tea

Let's talk more about that "cup of tea."

When I go out in the woods I want to be comfortable. I don't want to hike mountains in tennis shoes, or think that suffering is any part of the outdoor experience. Naw, there is just no reason for that.

I've learned to wear and take the right stuff for the trip and conditions. I am responsible for my well-being and enjoyment, and I take it seriously. I know what my pace is, I know what my comfort level is, and I treat myself right. Having served as a guide in Alaska, I can also take care of others if needed. However, guiding is a lot of work so I prefer to go out with friends who can take care of themselves. I like to get paid to guide or teach, as it's a whole different thing.

Tracking and bike riding are the two things that get me out several times a week. I have a lot to do, places to go, and things to check on. There are places that I go often to monitor the changes in wildlife use and simply to enjoy observing. Then there are days when I like to explore somewhere I haven't been before. The fascination just increases the more I learn about habitats and animals. After thirty-some odd years of tracking animals, I still have a lot to learn. The mysteries never cease.

Most of my days start with a plan. If I'm exploring, I study the map before I go and then take one with me. I usually go for day trips out of my home as I live next to a huge national forest. Thirty miles from my house in several directions gets me to spots where I don't see anyone else all day. I have a few select friends I go with who are as engaged with the adventures as I am, and whom I don't have to take care of in any way.

Once I have a plan—even if it's to not have a plan—I pack food, water, a stove or thermos for hot drinks, and everything I need to be comfortable. The weather dictates what's in my pack or in the saddlebags on my bike. If it's hot, that will include a neck cloth to wear wet around my neck, perhaps some ice in a thermos, and extra water. If it's cold, extra layers for every part of my body. If it's wet, rain pants, gaiters, and a good rain hat. I don't skimp on gear. I look for the best possible gear and shop carefully.

I once bought a raincoat and went to a nearby waterfall to test it. It didn't pass as I stood under the spray. I went back to the store that day and got another one. I find that, especially in women's gear, not all brands are equal. I think that boot and jacket manufacturers have thought in the past that women aren't really going to do it; that we might be more interested in how the stuff looks than what it can do. I realize that is changing now, as it should. But for a long time, this was a factor to keep in mind when shopping.

I also reserve the right to change my plans at any time. Things happen. And when they do, the best thing to do is just stop. And although I don't always literally drink tea, that's what I call taking a break.

When your outing gets tense, for whatever reason, sit down,

drink water, have a snack, sip some coffee out of the thermos, or brew a cup of tea. It's amazing how the emergencies find solutions with a mind that is refreshed. Unless someone is in immediate life-threatening danger, stopping works. I do it all the time.

~ Just Stop ~

One friend of ours (we'll call her Tony), who was riding bikes with us on a mission to see animal tracks on a back road, had heard that we stop for a cup of tea when things get tense. Apparently, she didn't really believe it.

The three of us were riding ebikes up a five-mile hill when Tony's bike stopped working well. It would cut out on her at odd times. Jane and I attempted to fix it. Her sensor wasn't working and I happened to have a spare in my toolkit. So we changed them out—except the one in my toolkit turned out to be broken as well. We were halfway to where we wanted to end up for the day. When her bike failed again, Tony generously volunteered to ride back to the cars and let us continue on. I suggested we stop for a cup of tea.

We all carry camp chairs on our bikes, so we broke them out and sat in the middle of the deserted road and sipped a hot drink. We listened to the birds and talked over the things we had seen so far and just enjoyed a relaxing break. At the end of it, Jane and I looked at each other and I knew we were on the same page. There was no way we were going to let our friend ride back by herself with an ailing bike.

Tony expressed amazement. "You actually do that! You actually stop for a cup of tea."

Yes, we do. And, knock on wood, we haven't let a bad decision made under stress ruin a day for us yet.

~ Other Essentials ~

Let's talk about the poncho. The poncho is one piece of gear I carry year-round. It's a place to sit, a shade, a shelter, a way to drag heavy things, a rain catcher, an emergency raincoat, an extra raincoat over one that has decided to leak. And it takes very little space in your pack.

Find a good one, preferably with a stuff-bag that keeps it small and organized. You can wear it in your kayak, tucked into your boat skirt, to keep you dry. Or use it to keep your bike and packs dry when you stop.

One caution though: if you wear a poncho riding a bike, it can cause a nasty crash if the corners get caught up in moving parts.

Space blankets are a thing, but I find two faults with them. One is that you don't use it when you should because they don't easily go back into their containers, and the other is that they deteriorate on their own without ever being used, so that you have to buy new ones all the time.

What about lights? Yes, you should always have a light with you, even if you are "just going out for a short day trip."

I once went on an exploration ride by myself off a trail from which I wanted to do an out-and-back trip. I had my map, my compass, and all my safety stuff—except for a light, because I still had some lessons to learn.

Well, mid-afternoon I got my map out and consulted it, intending to turn around at a certain point.

Only there was a problem. I was on the wrong side of the river.

I couldn't understand how that happened as I hadn't crossed any water. But the map showed the trail I was on located on the north side of the little fast-running creek. I couldn't see the creek, but I could hear it somewhere.

I decided to go down the trail a ways more, to see if I could figure out how I had gone wrong. I should have stopped for a cup of tea, as I then made a series of bad decisions.

When I had gone miles further down the steep trail than I planned on, I found the creek. The map insisted that it was in the wrong place, but I knew where I was because someone had put up a signpost to the various trails in the intersection. *Hummm...* I looked at the map again and decided I didn't want to ride up the steep trail I had just come down. I chose another one that went back towards my car. I was familiar with the top part of the trail and the road it came out on and how to get to my car from there.

When one thing goes wrong, another is sure to follow.

I got a good ways up my new trail when I started running into downed logs and forest debris blocking my way. I carried my bike over a few trees and walked some of it, thinking it would clear up and I could ride again. Wrong. It got worse.

By 8:30 p.m. I was exhausted, bleeding from various scrapes, hungry, and cold. I wasn't at the top of the trail yet and the thought of going back down over all those logs felt impossible. I realized that I might have to spend the night out. Darkness was due at 9:30 p.m. so I didn't stop, as I figured I couldn't waste any of my remaining daylight.

I can completely understand how emergencies happen.

They happen slowly, with several points where they could have gone differently.

At nine-thirty there was still a faint amount of light and I arrived at the trailhead on the road. I knew my car sat about two miles downhill on a logging road. I got on my bike and, riding the brakes, carefully tried to stay in the middle of the road. I was lucky. So lucky. I got to my car without a broken neck or limbs. I think I made it home about one-thirty in the morning.

If I had had a light, I could have slowed down and stayed safer. I escaped that time, but not because I did things right.

I don't forget things like that now when I pack for a day trip.

And, by the way, when I checked with someone who knew the area better than me, I found out that the map was wrong and had been for many years. As a matter of fact, GPS readings in the area have repeated the mistake as well.

~ One Cold Night ~

Another night I learned the importance of lights took place in early April. I was at a search and rescue team meeting when Susan James asked if anyone wanted to join her in fulfilling some owl-calling she needed to do. (Susan is a biologist who was counting owls for research.) I said I would, and she told me she needed to be at this remote spot around 10 p.m. I recall it was during a time that Mike worked evening banquets, so it wasn't a problem to go with her.

She planned to use a GPS to find the calling spot, so we loaded up our packs and started out around nine o'clock. We made it to the right place by ten but not easily. The snow was starting to melt and the wetlands we crossed had running water hidden under the snow. The result was that we would cross a snow bridge—and it would cave in. The two of us pretty much crashed in all the safe passages so that we couldn't go back the same way.

After Susan finished her requirements and logged her results, we had to figure out another way to get back to the car. But first, I had my stove so we drank a hot soup. Then we looked at the map and discovered a trail that would intercept the road we were parked on. It was a bit longer hike, but going back the same way we'd come was a sure way to get soaked and risk hypothermia.

As we set off, it started to snow. We tried to see with our headlamps but visibility was reduced. By some miracle, we found the trail, though, and thought we were at least halfway back.

By this time, it had grown a bit colder so we stopped for a hot drink. Good thing, too, as a little ways down the trail we discovered that the area was recently clear-cut and the trail obliterated. Of course, the map and GPS weren't able to give us that information.

The whole area featured "tree wells," which are deep holes around trees where the snow doesn't accumulate. When snow gets really slippery, you can fall into a tree well and there is nothing to stop you until you hit the trunk or stump. The warmish snow was super slippery. We helped each other out of tree wells and fell our way across the clear-cut debris in hopes of finding the trail on the other side. This was a long, slow, painful process, as we were determined not to get injured.

We were lucky neither of us got hurt. We were only bruised and scratched, cold and hungry. We used every warm thing to eat we found in our packs, stopping to fire up the stove several times.

When the trail became apparent again, although with slippery roots and more tree wells, it was well into the night. As a matter of fact, I remember saying, "Hey Susan, I have some bad news."

"What's that?"

"My batteries are about gone."

"Mine are too."

There was a silence as we moved slowly along and then I looked at my watch.

"Hey Susan, I have some good news."

"What's that?"

"It's gonna get light here in a few minutes." Indeed, it was about five a.m.

Just as the last of my headlamp blinked off, the sun appeared low on the horizon. Shortly after it got light, we made it to a meadow we recognized and only needed to get to the road without having to cross a substantial little creek that cut through the middle.

When we got to the road our car was parked on, we realized that my Mike and her boyfriend would have called search and rescue. We were both embarrassed to be the subject of a call-out. As we walked down the road, the Forest Service radio in the bottom of Susan's pack came alive. We heard one of our fellow rescuers trying to raise Susan on the radio. Though we could hear him, when she tried to answer the signal failed.

We were happy for the heater in the car as we headed back towards town. We decided to stop at the first house on the way, which was where the radio call had come from.

When we got there and knocked on the door, we were met with a very unhappy teammate. We never figured out which thing made him mad, our being caught out and not making it home all night, or, more likely, that the search group wasn't going to get to save us. They were ready to roll when we showed up.

The lessons from that night were many. We did several things right.

One of them was that we slowed way down when the going got hazardous. Even though it took us much longer than it should have, we were still walking when we got back. The second was that my little backpack stove and hot food were literally life savers. Each time we stopped for a hot drink, we also replenished our energy and relaxed.

As Mark Twain once said, "You can't be lost if you don't care where you are." Sometimes you need to stop and let go of the idea of being somewhere.

The map, the compass, and the GPS helped us, but those don't provide all the information you need. Our mistake, that of continuing when we realized how unstable the snow was, is a common one. Had we been on a stroll just for fun, we probably would have gone back as soon as we discovered the running water under the snow.

I think we both learned how much stamina it takes and how to manage your energy in case of further bad developments. Neither one of us wanted to press our luck, and as a result, we made it.

It's good to know that you can spend the night out and not die or get hurt. The challenge might be tedious at times, but it is quite doable.

~ 17 ~

The Inner Voices

It's time to talk about your five-year-old. We all still have our five-year-old selves inside of us and they come out once in a while.

They are the voice that says, "Wait till they hear what I had to go through, then they'll feel sorry for me."

Or, "Somebody will rescue me."

Or, "I just can't do it. I'm going to sit down right here until they come to get me."

The five-year-old talks in a sulk and feels sorry for itself. It's a victim and it's really all someone else's fault. They tend to come out when you are tired, cold, hungry, too hot and sweaty, thirsty, and itchy.

The best way to deal with this infant in you is to recognize it and take care of it. Baby it for a bit, but don't let it make decisions. The adult in the room has to step up when the pity party is over.

Sometimes you might have to recognize this five-year-old in others. Often you can just wait and they will deal with it and the adult will return. At least I hope so, for your sake.

If you are by yourself and want to make good decisions, learn to sort out advice from your five-year-old and from another character I have lately started calling Mrs. Beasley. Mrs. Beasley also talks in a recognizable, condescending voice that comes from a talking doll with the same name made by Mattel. In your mind, however, her message might be that you are no good, too old, too out of shape, and that you can't do that. That you aren't up to the task and never have been.

"You shouldn't go there, dear, you might slip and fall."

"Gee thanks, Mrs. Beasley, but I have my walking stick and I want to see those tracks…so back off!"

If you've injured yourself in the past, Mrs. Beasley might become a constant companion until you get your confidence back.

What you really should listen to is your intuition and the facts you have gathered that you can count on.

For instance, intuition is when you are tracking someone or something and you come to a realization such as, "This person is favoring a right leg." There have been clues all along but it was your subconscious that gathered them.

The realization of these clues might come together quickly, though sometimes it is hard to verbalize them without some passage of time. If you find yourself thinking, "I have a feeling …," examine it and see if there were subtle clues that led you to it.

I don't blindly trust intuition, but I do listen and make note. Sometimes further observations bear it out and other times it leads you to a dead end.

The freedom to make your own decisions is important, but you need the self-discipline to know which of your decisions are based on rational thought and not a product of emotional reactions.

It's kind of like we are all in a canoe, bumping down a river, and each of us holds a paddle. It's up to us to pick up our own paddle and steer our own canoe and decide, "What is the best line to follow to keep from being overturned?"

The mental discipline it takes to be a good tracker is much the same. There are ways to observe evidence and come to solid conclusions, and then there are ways to self-sabotage. You can look at a story on the ground and decide that only a bear could make such a mess, but then, maybe it's just a busy squirrel digging up last fall's stashes.

This kind of inner dialogue is a classic tracker dilemma that can show up in the evaluation process that CyberTracker uses. For example, the tracker sees a sign or track and immediately determines who made it, only to follow up that thought with a long, involved, mental assessment that talks the tracker right out of the first impression and, sometimes, into a wrong answer. The pressure to come up with a right answer can pull a virtual shade down over the tracker's eyes and mind.

On one evaluation I took, I was shown an impression in the dirt and asked who left it. I glanced at it and saw the oblong, crescent-shaped depression of the metacarpal pad a bear paw leaves. There was no sign of digits or claw marks, but that shape is pretty distinctive. Based on the area we were in, I answered "black bear" and moved on.

I was amazed that the other trackers took so long over it. I went back to look at it again. But then, maybe it was a deer track that got messed up when the animal slipped in the mud? Maybe it was a bird making a bad landing, or possibly human sign, like someone slipped and put their hand down? I almost talked myself out of my original answer. But this was one instance I was able to release the feeling of pressure and stick to my first answer. I was correct.

Sometimes, when you see animal sign in the wild, it might take weeks, months, or years before it makes sense to you. Trackers can hang on to a wrong answer and even teach it to someone else. Or, they can have an epiphany and put clues together like, "Oh! The reason that the new coyote scat is here and part of it is way down the road is this elk track! The elk kicked it!"

Epiphany is fun. Like when a new student is pondering a depression in the dirt and someone else comes along and picks up the rock and puts it back into its nest. That usually only happens once.

Focus lock can happen to all of us at any time. Say you're driving and you see a bright blue thing on the side of the road. For a moment you stare at it to the exclusion of all other input until your mind can put a name to it. Horses are famous for focusing on one small, scary thing, like the corner of a bridge, and they won't cross, their eyes fixed on this thing they don't understand.

Our mind plays tricks on us every day. Another mental hazard I've found is the lazy mind.

When I was guiding and someone would ask me for instance, "What is that bird?" and I would tell them the name of the bird, their minds would immediately shift elsewhere, as it had a name and what more do you need? They probably wouldn't remember it, either.

But if they asked me and I returned with another question, such as, "What is it doing?" then they would have to think a bit.

In one case the bird was an American Dipper. After I asked

what it was doing, the guest observed carefully, then he said, "A break dance on the rocks." When I finally told him it was a Dipper, he probably never forgot it.

Some people can tell if people are lying and others cannot. They might hear two different versions of the same incident and not be able to examine the evidence to see who is right. Tracking relies on solid clues that you can touch, photograph, and see again in another spot. The danger is in single-factor reasoning.

For instance, one tracker sees a paw print with four digits but no claw marks and determines that it has to be a feline because feline tracks don't normally show claws.

Another tracker comes along and says it is canine because the negative space between the pad and digits make a clear X shape and it has an overall oval shape, the two leading digits are aligned, the digits one and four are pulled in close to a small metacarpal pad, and that pad is small compared to the area the toes take up, and the substrate is too coarse to show claws anyway.

The tracker with the more solid reasons for the determination is correct. The mental discipline to sort these things out is yet another benefit of learning to track.

Then there is the "Hell if I know," pronounced "Ellifino" animal. (Thank you Rob Speiden for this one.) To be a good tracker you have to be able to be wrong, wrong, wrong, or, just not know. People in Western cultures develop a healthy ego that makes them afraid of being wrong. Being wrong, though, is part of the fun. It's a good way to learn and it's a good lesson for those around you.

Once Jane let me go on about a scat we found in the melting

snow. It was tubular with a large diameter and a good volume and I was imagining the big wolf that left it. Unfortunately, out loud. Because minutes later, when I picked up a small stick and poked it, out came dog kibble.

Oops.

The bottom line is, if you are physically fit enough to travel in the wild, you also need to cultivate a fit mind. It's okay to be emotional, but it's not healthy to base decisions on emotions. Even mild ones. Like hoping you find wolf sign so much that everything looks like wolf tracks. So going out for hikes, riding bikes or horses, and traveling in the wilderness makes you physically fit—and learning to track can help make you mentally fit.

~ 18 ~

When to Lie

All solo adventurers need to think about one particular consideration: if you're alone, you might become a target of other humans.

Every kind of mischief possible can come your way, whether you are man or woman, big or small, weak or strong. Right up to and including murder, unfortunately there are humans who think they can take advantage of a lone traveler.

For years I tracked by myself. Part of my routine to keep myself safe includes my trailhead procedures:

I park away from the trailhead if possible.

I examine any cars that are present.

I look for tracks, feel the heat from the hood of the vehicle to judge time, and glance in to see what was left behind, what stickers they display, and how many people were in the car.

The biggest track anyone can leave is their vehicle. If someone looks my car over, they will find my driver's seat all the way back, no sign that a woman drives the car (like ponytail holders or makeup). Instead they'll see a can of Grizzly chew on my console, as well as some bullets. (A can I found discarded on the trail.) I paste no political or environmental stickers on my car and hang no fuzzy little animals from the mirror. (I keep waiting for the guys who fix my car to ask about the chew can and bullets but so far they haven't.)

When I have assessed the trailhead and the possible people I might meet, sometimes I leave and go somewhere else. Most of the time, I am lucky enough to be the only one there. If I determine that there are a couple of bird watchers, perhaps a man and woman up the trail by the tracks they left, I will still go. Three other bikes, no worries. Three guys with a dog… umm, maybe not.

I'm an honest person. I really don't like to lie because then you have to remember what you said, but there is one situation where lying is called for. If I am on my own in the back country and I run into someone who insists on talking to me, I lie. When they ask if I am alone, of course I'm not.

I realize that this unease is not shared by some of the men I know, but it would still pay for you to think about this. If nothing else, it may give you an insight into what your woman friends and/or employees have to consider.

One evening while Mike was working his banquet job, I decided to walk up a nearby trail that has a great view of the Columbia River and eat my supper up there. It was a beautiful summer night. After my soup and sandwich, I started the hike back down. I could hear people coming up the trail. Men, in fact. This particular trail is narrow, with a cliff on the uphill side as you descend, and it drops off steeply on the other side. I would have to pass them.

As they got closer, I realized there also might be a little beer involved. They were huffing and puffing and joking profanely as they approached me. I stood aside in a wide spot so they could pass.

But they didn't. The leader stopped and, after looking me up and down, asked me how far it was to a flat spot where they could camp. I gave directions to the nearest trail crossing which had a camp spot.

The second in line piped up, "Hey, are you up here by yourself?"

"Of course not!" I said. "Didn't you see my husband? Long white beard, wearing camo and carrying a rifle?"

"Naw, we didn't see anyone."

I pushed by. "Well, all I can say is watch your back. He loves to play games with people."

They all stepped aside and were quiet. I glanced at the two guys at the end of the line and they looked a bit nervous.

Remember that. You are never alone if anyone asks, no matter what you have to make up. Your friends are meeting you; you're on a search training mission and the dogs will be finding you soon; or, "Can you tell my friends behind that I will be waiting for them at the next trail crossing?"

"You shouldn't be out here without a gun," is another one I get all the time.

My answer?

"What makes you think I'm unarmed?"

I've asked Mike what kinds of things he thinks are dangerous for solo men. He spends his time at the beach surfing, or wing-foiling on the Columbia River. He told me there are situations to avoid, and that being aware of brewing trouble can forestall becoming involved. Sometimes out in the surf you can feel a certain vibe that someone is looking for a fight. Surf protocols have been hammered out over the years: who gets the next wave, when you can share a wave and when you'd better not, and how to avoid each other when you are paddling out. Unfortunately, not everyone goes out with respect and willingness to share. Fistfights on the beach and violence in the water can happen. Mike says a good defense is to just leave for a while; head to another part of the break or call it a day.

Men have different challenges than women for sure, but one of the things women deal with is the impulse of men to help you, even if you don't need it. Sometimes it's downright good-natured, and other times it's a form of disrespect.

Just last week I pulled into one of my near-but-not-on-the-trail parking spots to wait for my tracking partner. I always park facing out for a quick getaway, and by the way, I always carry extra keys. My bike was on my rack and I was standing by my car when a guy on an ATV pulled up next to me and stopped. He turned off the motor.

"Just wanted to let you know we saw a cougar up here."

I smiled to myself. Yup, here was another guy trying to scare me. He must have seen a woman by herself getting ready for a bike ride and thought it was his duty to make sure I was worried.

For sure his intentions might have been simple concern, as he probably was afraid of cougars. But whether he intended it or not, his comment was based on an assumption predicated by my gender.

"Cool!" I said. "I love cougars! What a special experience it must have been to see one. They are magnificent animals. I track them all the time but rarely get to lay eyes on one. I'm so excited there is still one here...they're so good for the habitat."

I wish I had a photo of the look on his face.

He did stick around for a while as I told him a little bit about cougar ecology, how they actually form helpful family groups and feed protein to all the other little animals, while they keep the herds active and healthy. He seemed to soak up my information so I just kept going until his wife drove up looking for him. She didn't want to listen to me. Oh well.

Another time I drove my little Subaru and bike up to a ridge I call Bear Alley because lots of huckleberries grow there. As I got to where I wanted to park and got my bike out, a truck pulled in next to me. The guys in the truck told me I probably didn't want to go for a ride, as they had just seen a huge male bear an hour before.

I got my bike out anyway and told them thanks for their concern but I wasn't particularly worried. They stayed, trying to talk me out of riding for "my own good."

I patiently explained that I had been a bear-viewing guide in Alaska for four summer seasons, taking people in the back-country to see grizzly/brown bears, and had even written a book about it.

Then they said they had called their buddies who were bear hunters and they were on their way up the hill to kill this big trophy bear.

Because they drove away after that, I went on my bike ride.

A little way into the ride, I picked up the tracks of a medium-sized adult black bear, with a four-and-a-half-inch-wide front track. The bear was walking down the road stepping in the soft dust and leaving clear tracks. I got off my bike and wiped them out. When I heard another truck coming down the road, this time a diesel, I picked up my bike and climbed up to a spot where I could watch and stay out of sight. But the men from the truck weren't even looking for tracks. As a matter of fact, they were staring straight ahead.

The guys went by slowly, one driving, one in the back with the rifle ready, and one in the passenger seat with a rifle sticking out the window. Definitely not a fair chase tactic.

They went down the road for a few miles and then I heard them turn around. I wasn't in a hurry to go anywhere so I stayed put, quietly eating huckleberries. It's illegal to interrupt a legal hunt and even though they were hunting from a truck, it would be their word against mine if I stopped them or scared off the bear. So I just stayed out of sight in a spot I knew would be hard to shoot at.

The truck came back and the guys stayed in it. When the sound faded from the truck, I heard the bear, which had been up the same hill I was on. It went crashing down to the road, over the side, and down into a deep, steep jungle of vegetation and trees that I don't know how a human could even attempt to navigate. When I came down the hill, there were the truck tracks, and on top of the tire tread were the tracks of the bear. I'm sure the bear eluded them easily, as did I.

Not too many people can track. Mostly because they don't look. It isn't hard to elude someone, especially if they are driving. When you are quiet, you can hear someone coming from a long ways away. It gives you time to take evasive actions.

If you go off the road or trail and into some brush and shadow, making sure you don't have a reflective surface visible, like possibly your watch, you are really hard to detect. Unless your friends are trackers, of course.

I find that I don't have to be conscious of hiding my trail

when I do this, as most people can walk by and not see you, even if you are in plain sight.

My general rule for meeting people in the back country is that they can see me once but they won't see me a second time, nor will they know which way I went or where I am parked. Most people don't care, which is great. They say hello and don't expect to see you again. There are, however, some people who just want to see how much trouble they can cause someone else. It's best if you never give them the chance.

The best way I can explain it is: Don't be obedient. Don't be helpful. And don't let someone else interrupt or ruin your day. Lie, and be downright rude if you have to. If you are alone, you need to take care of yourself, and that means staying alone.

There was a horrible story in Washington state about a mother and daughter who were abused and murdered on a trail. One of the investigators was a friend of mine (a fellow tracker) and he knows I go alone and encourage others to do the same. He was traumatized by what happened to these women and asked me to pass on a message to all the other females who travel the back country. It was that you don't have to do what a man tells you, and you don't have to help them.

One day I was riding a main back road to get to my remote turnoff and guy in a small car, who was coming the opposite direction, stopped and rolled down his window. I didn't look at him but rode on by. Out of the corner of my eye, I profiled him and his car. Nope.

Perhaps he just wanted directions and I was being incredibly rude, but I rode on down the road until I was out of sight. Then I pushed my bike up a creek drainage where I was out of sight of the road and decided to take a break.

The man turned around and drove back looking for me. I watched as he drove by, slowly. He turned again and drove back by, looking, but didn't see me. Again, maybe he was innocently looking for directions, but I never really feel like taking that chance. After all, it is my day, and why should I interrupt it for someone else? I waited about half an hour and he didn't come back, so I got back on the road and made it to my turnoff without seeing anyone. I didn't see anyone else the rest of the day.

Now that I am older and I have some gray hair, I don't get as much of the same kind of attention I got when I was younger. That suits me fine. I also probably exude a bit more confidence and danger. I keep a can of bear-size pepper spray easily visible on my handlebars where I can shoot it while riding. Most people who want to strike up a conversation in the wilderness notice this right away. It isn't there for wild animals, but for humans. I would have no qualms in spraying down someone who wanted to block me or detain me.

Years ago, when I was a County Welfare worker in San Diego, my job was to interview people who needed help and get them what they needed. It was usually safe, but not always. Because some women in the department had experienced some problems with clients in closed interview rooms, we invited police officers to come in and offer us training. One of the most amazing things to me was that when the male police officer, who was wearing padding, asked the women to hit him...they couldn't do it. How did we get raised to be *so* nice?

Think about your ability to hit someone, ignore someone, or evade someone. Would you do it half-heartedly, or would you put your all into it? You must develop a code and a line that can't be crossed. You don't have to be polite. I know I already said that. It needs to be said again. And your gender doesn't matter for this advice. If someone seeks to interrupt your day, you just don't have to play.

Look at it this way. You are enjoying your day alone and have the ultimate freedom to do whatever you want. It's a hard-won freedom and days are precious. No one has the right to interrupt you and make their reality your priority. There are times to help people, but those times should be reserved for when that's your purpose. Like if you are part of a search and rescue group. But even there, you need to learn to take care of yourself.

One of the lessons learned the hard way in search and rescue is that you need to put yourself first, or you can't help anyone. The ability to help others comes from competence and strength.

One day guiding in the cold and rain, I was driving a group of passengers in an open boat in Alaska. One of the men was particularly unprepared and he asked me for my jacket. I declined. I was, after all, in charge of the boat and everyone on it. Had I become hypothermic and made bad decisions, it could have been much more serious. Instead, I made sure we headed to the dock as soon as we could so he could go up to the lodge and get warm. He subsequently tried to get me fired. Fortunately, my boss at the time agreed with me that making him comfortable at my loss was not a bright idea.

If you are in a group, everyone has everything they need, and you run across someone needing help and you can do so without putting your group as risk, by all means give help and aid as you can. If you can't help, you can go to find cell service and call for help.

If you are by yourself, it's a whole different ballgame and

you totally need to take of yourself as a first priority. Then if you can help, do so. Just don't do more harm.

A snowy back road offered just enough clearing that I could drive to one of the spots I wanted to check for an elk herd. I hiked in and found what I wanted. But on my way back I spotted a truck in a ditch. The truck was damaged and would not be going anywhere soon. There was a guy sitting on the hillside just above it.

I stopped, as it was late afternoon and about to get cold. I rolled my window down an inch or so and yelled out to him that I was going to the nearest cell reception site and would call the sheriff. I asked if he had a jacket and he nodded, but he didn't say anything. I looked at the situation and realized what a mess he was in, and that helping him would put me in one too.

When I got hold of the county sheriff's dispatch office, I gave them road numbers and the exact location. The dispatcher asked me if I could give the guy a ride. I explained that I was by myself and the answer was a definite NO. I did leave my phone number and name, as the reporting party.

Later, a deputy called and thanked me and said there were drugs and guns involved, as well as a subject who needed to be subdued.

Can you imagine what might have happened if I opened my car to this person?

Okay, you get the idea. You are number one and don't you forget it. I want you to enjoy what wilderness has to offer and take care of yourself. You can do it.

~ 19 ~

Camping

Heading out to the wild for a while is a whole different thing from doing day trips. The rewards of camping are that you get to be out there at the very beginning of the day when the stars start to fade and the dew comes down heavy. It's one of the two times of day that most people miss but the animals enjoy. It's the time they move from one feeding area to another, and the morning chorus of birds sweeps the landscape from east to west.

Walking at that time of day seems spiritual. Early morning and dusk are called crepuscular times, and many animal species are most active at those times. If you just sit and watch as shadows form, you can see why. There is much less human interference in most places at daybreak.

Tracking in the early hours can yield some interesting sign. Furry animals moving through the brush will leave a dry trail on the bushes, or if they cross a road, they may leave moisture drops from dripping wet fur, as well as prints of wet, soft paws. It's easier to age the tracks in different substrates based on how much dew there has been, or how little. It's always fun to put your fingers delicately into the morning track of a black bear and think about the bear that was just there.

Most people who camp love to have campfires. It's a built-in response to being in the wild. The smoke and the fire, as well as people sitting around and talking, singing, and telling stories is pretty much what you would expect. You can see each other and the fire, but beyond that is the empty, dark, forbidding wilderness. I believe this is the time when animals get to do their people watching. They can move all around the humans in the dark without being seen.

~ Night Hike ~

A night hike without flashlights is a good way to experience the wild at night. One camping evening, a friend of mine and I decided to hike a ridge trail near our camp. As we made our way there, right where the trail left the road, we discovered a group of guys camping. They were gathered around a big fire. It was a still night, so we could hear them talking as we walked down the road near the camp. I paused and listened to the chatter.

They were afraid. Their guns were propped up next to them where they sat on logs. I grew concerned that, if they heard us moving, they would lift up the rifles and shoot at the sound. Because we really wanted to hike the trail, I yelled out, letting them know we were going to walk through the camp.

They told us that a cougar had been sighted on the trail and we shouldn't go up there. But, of course, it was a cougar I had tracked before, kind of a shy being that never seemed to leave a small area. We went up the trail. It was a beautiful night up on the ridge and we could see the view in the moonlight.

When we came back down, I let the camp know again. There

was only one man left sitting up. It seemed they were going to take turns doing a watch all night. As we walked back to our camp, my friend asked me what was wrong with me that I wasn't afraid when grown men had to set a watch. That's a good question, I guess. For some reason, I was way more afraid of the men with guns because they were spooked. The cougar I could count on to be reasonable.

One night, when I was attending a human tracking class in Oregon at a remote camp, most of the students were headed to town on Saturday night and I was left staring at a young man who was a forensic entomology tracker. Someone in the class had explained to me that he was involved in the discovery that maggots leave dead human bodies en masse at certain points of decomposition, which was an important factor in solving cold crimes. Apparently, in cases where the detectives thought the body had been moved it wasn't always the case, because maggots leave a trail that looks like a body being dragged.

Only the two of us remained in an empty camp. He asked me if I wanted to see his body slides from the dead body farm he had just come back from. I didn't. (I admit I was chicken.)

For those of you like my editor who've never heard the term, a dead person farm is where forensic scientists study how long it takes bodies to decompose—bodies generously donated to science to help crime fighters.

Instead we took a hike.

It was dusk when we started out. We looked for tracks and got involved in a trail that took us across a creek. When it grew dark, we left our flashlights off to see how well we could get our night vision to kick in. It was a moonlit night so hiking was pretty easy. He said he knew of a bridge we could cross to travel back across the creek, and that would make a nice loop walk. Only when we arrived, we found a group of people camping right on the bridge with a big fire in the middle. Their vehicles blocked the whole road.

We probably could have walked through their camp but they were whooping it up, playing with guns, and throwing their beer cans over the side. Neither one of us was keen to start up a conversation with them. We walked pretty close to the camp and they didn't see us. The fire made a wall of darkness. We got close enough to hear their conversation and still they were unaware.

Using hand signals, we decided to cross the creek. The water was low and the sound of the water covered our movements, but the campers were making too much noise to hear us anyway. They didn't detect us. But it was too much for my friend. He just had to do it. He let out one of the loudest and most perfect wolf howls.

The camp went absolutely still. We didn't move either. They directed powerful spotlights all around themselves but by that time there were bushes between us and their lights. We outwaited them and they started talking again. It was clear we had spooked them.It was hard to keep from laughing as we made our way to the road and walked softly away.

So I'm not a big fan of the campfire. Instead, I like to do a quiet sit. After dinner, instead of gathering around a fire, I like to spread out and have each person take a spot looking outward. An hour of observation at that time of night yields some very interesting sounds. Then, when everyone gets back to camp, they have a story to tell and sometimes they are pretty dang interesting.

~ Trade-offs ~

There are many ways to camp. Watching folks camp in Baja, I have noticed that people start out in tents, or sleeping in the back of their car or van. Then they move up to a pop-top camper, or a truck camper. After that, it's a small motor home or trailer. Then it's a big motor home or a big fifth wheel. Then, they start downsizing again. It's a cycle. And it's always a balance between drivability and livability. Something that is easy to drive isn't very livable and a big rig with lots of amenities is really hard to drive, and limited in where it can go.

Some try the idea of a trailer that you can park somewhere and then you have a car. However, that leaves you in a situation where it isn't fast to leave if you need to. A big motor home leaves you vulnerable to theft unless you camp in an established camp. A four-wheel-drive truck camper can get you to some cool places, but most of the time if you have to drive away at night, you need to get out of the camper and climb in the truck. A small motor home can leave in the middle of the night if someone harasses you, but if you put the canopy and chairs out, that advantage is gone. A van camper can be very mobile and safe, but hanging out inside for a long time can be tedious.

When you go to buy a recreational vehicle, they'll ask you what kind of camping you want to do. If you don't know, you often buy something and then it dictates what kind of camping you will do.

I sure haven't found the perfect answer yet, but in the sixteen or so years I have spent the winters camping in Baja I have learned a few things.

One is that there really isn't such a thing as "free" camping.

No matter where you are, you are on somebody's land. Your security and safety depend on the local people wanting you to be there. So if you find a cool place to camp on a remote beach, find a local and ask whose land it is. Then go to that person or family and ask permission, offer some money, and ask if there is anything you should know. Then there will also be someone to talk to if you have a problem. I found that in Baja, the family who lets you stay on their land also has a tendency to protect "their gringos" from the other locals.

I really like being "self-contained," which means I don't have to use someone else's bathroom and we don't need to hook up to power. Water is acquired the same way you get groceries, by going to local stores. In each location, the local customs and set up are different and if you are nice, kind, and think about what others need, you will find that people welcome you and help you. Especially if you don't leave a mess. After all, if you like the place, they do too.

One little town we go to has a long history of surfers camping there. Surfers are usually a bunch of guys. A few of them live such disorganized lives that only a dog can put up with them. The town has been amazingly tolerant of these feckless nomads who bring drugs, alcohol bingeing, and attitudes of selfishness into their little village. It's probably due to the fact that they leave a little money behind, and that not all of them are pigs. Some of them are downright saints. Among the surfers are firemen and medical professionals who make a difference when they visit. And, surfers have a tendency to police their own crowd. They can throw someone out of the area for being too out there.

And lately, women surfers have started to travel on their

own. They live more organized lives, for the most part. Some of them are world-class athletes and don't put up with much from anyone.

Traveling alone where there are other people means you need to think out your situation ahead of time. Can you leave quickly at any time? Do you have a plan for your comfort and peace without relying on others? I spend a lot of time in the wilderness by myself, but when I go to Baja, it's necessary to be more social. For me, the key is in knowing when to leave a situation. Your whole relationship with human beings needs the same kind of scrutiny you give your relationships with wild animals.

You can ask the same questions:

Does this person need something from me?

Is it something I can give easily, and if I do give, will they then demand more?

What kind of energy is this person or are these people generating?

Is it good, or do I need a raincoat here?

The bottom line, like always, is to take care of yourself, do no harm to others, but don't let them harm you either. And in that I mean mental, emotional, fiscal, or physical harm. It's easy to just go along and put up with some stuff from others, but you'll live a longer, happier life if you draw the line and keep it. One of the wonderful things about traveling is meeting new people, and it can also be one of the bummers. The nice guy on the beach can get ugly after some pills and beers. Until you know someone well enough, camp accordingly, so that their life doesn't become your problem.

If you are traveling with another person and you are uncomfortable with the situation you run into, make sure your partner will trust your opinion.

Once on a surf trip with a friend, some famous surfers showed up from Hawaii. Unfortunately, they started being rude to a local vender. Venders live there and they all know each other. While the guys were teasing the daughter and insulting her father, I saw her brother sneak away and head off running. I asked my friend if we could leave. She said yes, but not before she berated the surf stars for being buttheads.

We broke camp and got on the road. The stories you hear from people who have been robbed and harassed in a foreign country are interesting. Just like people do with wild animals, there isn't anyone to tell the other side of the story. I hope those guys weren't harmed, but it would be too much of a coincidence if they had gear stolen in the middle of the night. You just don't insult the local population of either animals or people and expect that you will be safe and go home with all your gear and money.

~ Site Considerations ~

Picking a camp site is as important as buying a house. Where you lay your head and set up your life makes a difference in your experience. Even in a campground, careful selection can make a difference. If you are in the wild, it can mean the difference between life and death. I usually have a whole list of things to consider when we go to a new place.

One of the things that I look for is a place I can leave, if needed, even in the dark. The wind direction, shade or sun, and the ability to hear well are also important. A view is nice, but not at the expense of having to camp close to other people. Camping next to a stream or pounding surf can be a handicap, especially if you are sleeping on the ground. The noise of the water can keep you from hearing important things. Plus, everyone wants to be on the cliff edge so they can see the sunrise, or just at the water's edge so they can simply walk out for a swim. The cliff edge can get real exciting in a lightning storm and the water has a tendency to not stay where it's supposed to all night. It's just plain more comfortable to be a little distance from the most attractive feature.

Last year on the way south, Mike and I drove thirteen miles up a dirt road off the main path to camp in a BLM camp that we'd heard was pretty cool. When we got there, we found a few people already camped. We drove our camper over the cattle guard and into a large corral, completely fenced off. I took one look and said, "No way! You could be so easily trapped in here while bandits did whatever they wanted to you." We crossed that one off the list.

There are two theories about camping on the ground around wild animals. One is to put yourself in deep brush like a rabbit, and the other is to camp on a rise with clearing all around. The theory about the deep brush camp is that animals would have to make noise and be real determined to interrupt your sleep. The reasoning behind the clearing, and maybe on a small rise, is that animals would have to leave the cover of the trees and brush to get to you. Keep that in mind, as not all habitats offer these choices. Make the best of the area you're in.

There are also new things to consider, like the portable electric fence now available for campers and backpackers. Bears can feel that an electric fence is on without touching it. A good night's sleep in Alaska, free from being rumbled by bears or stepped on by moose, might be worth the cost of one of these.

If you've learned to track, picking a campsite becomes much easier. "Off the beaten track" may be a cliche, but it's also practical camping advice.

~ 20 ~

Without a bathroom

Treesong Nature Awareness and Retreat Center held a tracking class for women on mountain bikes one summer. Jane Doudney helped me teach it and it was a fun outing in a remote place.

We started with what a woman needs to know to take care of a bike and how to equip herself for a ride. Then we took off together on a closed road.

We stopped at the top of the first half-mile hill to let everyone catch up. I usually use this time to let the city energy dissipate and for everyone to realize that they are now out in nature time. We talked about how to proceed—not talking but observing—and how we were going to ride at a steady, slower pace. I asked if there were any questions. From the back, I heard a small, quiet voice.

"Umm, so how do you pee out here?"

Yes, I'd heard that right. She was serious, too. Even though everyone kind of laughed at first, they all were paying attention for an answer.

I put the kickstand down on my bike and stepped out where they could see me.

"If you want to be comfortable in the woods, you need to be comfortable heeding nature's call. After all, it is a proven fact that you can't think if you have to pee."

They laughed nervously.

"Just let us know, like saying 'I have to go find a tree,' or 'I'm going to go empty my holding tank,' or 'I need to mark my territory.' As a tracker, you know better than to leave any physical sign like a Kleenex or toilet paper, so carry a Ziplock bag. Actually, two of them works well, one with paper in it and another inside to put the used ones into."

Another woman asked, "But what if you don't have a handy little plastic bag of TP?"

"Well," I took a breath. "Then you need to know what your favorite leaves are. Personally, I like mullein, moss, old man's beard lichen, and my favorite is snow."

There was a long pause as they digested this information and then another quiet question, "But how do you keep from getting it on you?"

I still had their undivided attention, some of them probably wanting to know the answer and others wondering how I was gonna get out of that one.

I decided to demonstrate. "First, find a spot where you feel comfortable taking down your pants and look at the plants to check for poison oak or thorns. If not, feel which way the wind is blowing on your face." I turned towards to the wind to show them. "I usually ask a friendly branch to hold my little bag for me."

I put my bag in a branch by my bike.

"Next, keeping the wind in your face, pull your pants down and then reach between your legs and grab the back of your pants and hold them close to you."

I pulled down my pretend pants and showed them the reach move.

It was quiet. No one seemed to have anything to add.

No one in that class brought up the serious issue of defecation in the woods, as we were all there only for the day. But if you are planning an overnight trip or longer, don't think you'll just figure it out when you get there, or leave the arrangement up to someone else! There is a whole book on subject that I highly recommend, *How to Shit in the Woods,* 4th Edition; *An Environmentally Sound Approach to a Lost Art* by Kathleen Meyer.

I suggest planning ahead. These days there are even more ways of safely taking care of this. I no longer worry about it because I now have a camper with a bathroom, which I dearly love. However, I've had my missteps and mishaps in the days before our current camper.

Since you can study a whole book's worth of information on the subject, I'm going to stick to an emergency method for when you are caught without preplanning.

First, it is absolutely essential to dig a hole. Eight inches deep is about minimum.

Second, baby wipes really help, but you can't leave them behind.

And, most important, if you are not used to squatting, make yourself a seat with rocks or branches and test it first.

Whatever you do, try not to have it be an emergency.

I realize that we all get sick once in a while and messes happen, but make it easy on yourself with a little preparation so that you don't have a big mess to clean up. When you are done, no one should be able to tell you were there. Basically, leave no trace.

You might consider some new products, such as a small

backpack that includes a folding toilet with a system of biodegradable bags that you can take home with you, or dispose of safely when you have the opportunity. Look them up on the internet. If you are camping for a few days, it would be really worth it to have your own system. Nothing can ruin a day in the woods easier than having to deal with a natural function in a less than comfortable way.

I remember one great surf spot in Baja that I had always wanted to visit. Mike and I owned a pop-top camper then, without the bathroom, and we camped in the sand dunes by the ocean. It was beautiful, with great surf. It wasn't until the next morning that I discovered the problem with the place. There was an outhouse, but after peeking in the door, I realized that it would be less traumatic to visit a plane crash. Then I tried the secluded dune method. I figured I could dig a hole pretty easily. But as I walked, I could see that no one else had dug a hole, removed their toilet paper, or cleaned up after themselves, and everyone who'd been there in the past weeks clearly avoided the outhouse. It was a truly sh*tty place.

After that, I did an internet search and found a system we could use in the camper. But it wasn't too long before we both agreed on a hard-sided camper, which wasn't susceptible to high winds and blowing dust, with a toilet and shower.

It's not like I didn't experience my years in a tent. Backpacking and car camping are some of the easiest and most available ways to get out.

When I used to tent camp, I found out quickly that a two-person tent is just about perfect for one. Two people in one of those have to be pretty close for it to be comfortable. And sometimes that is a way to get close to someone you want to be close with. But you'd better be sure about that.

I also developed my systems for dealing with campground bathrooms. I carried an opaque shopping bag with a spray bottle of bleach solution for cleaning the bathroom before I used it. Over the years that bag expanded to contain a pee bucket, which I emptied in the bathroom in the morning instead of having to go walking around in the dark seeking the bathroom. I used a food storage container that sealed well and simply rinsed it out and sprayed it with my bleach solution.

I have also used sun showers; the clear bags with a black backing that heat up during the sunny part of the day. Most of them include a plastic shower head and you can just hang them up and get wet, turn it off, soap up, then turn it on again and rinse off. We found that if you can add a little boiled water just before you take a shower it works really well. The other factors are wind and privacy. They make shower tents now just for that purpose, but a little engineering and a couple of tarps can make a sun shower downright pleasant.

These are all things you need to ask about if you are going with a group. How will you poop, pee, and what do we do with garbage? Will we have showers and what are they like? How will we cook and wash dishes? Will there be hot water and how do we store food? What do we do in the event of a storm, and can I leave at any time?

In the spirit of taking care of yourself so that you have fun and are able to spread the fun around, you can't leave these things to chance.

If you're working in the outdoors, these are questions you shouldn't be shy about asking. If you're the boss, make sure your crew is taken care of.

Many a guided outdoor adventure is run by college kids who might have no experience in providing life comforts. Lots of times a trip on a river or a mountain sounds like a great time, but if the details aren't taken care of, you can end up miserable. Especially if you've been a solo adventurer who has learned to be self-sufficient and are suddenly in the hands of others who put you in awkward situations. Be wary.

~ 21 ~

What's in That Pack?

One of the fun things we did in search and rescue was to hold a pack night. Along with generous snacks to keep us going, we would empty our packs on the meeting room table and see what everyone else's contained that were cool gadgets and things to keep us safe and comfortable.

Some of the memorable items were paraffin-soaked dryer lint balls to use for fire starting and all kinds of knives, pack saws, and first-aid kits. Everyone had a different idea about snack foods. They had to be resilient and able to withstand waiting in a pack for many hours before consumption.

One of my favorites was what I called an apple ball. I would take a whole apple, slice it into at least sixteenths, and put it back together with a slice of cheese between the wedges. Then I would wrap the whole thing in foil, so it would form a ball. The round shape helped it fit into the pack in spots where other things didn't. It sure tasted good around two a.m. on overnight searches.

Packs are constantly evolving things. Every new piece of gear you get needs to have a purpose, and things you never use need to come out.

Every change of season has different requirements, as well. A winter pack is quite different from a summer one. My current packs are the saddle bags I use on my bike.

In search and rescue, the big question was whether your pack was sufficient for you to be comfortable for at least twenty-four hours in the field. Now that I travel mostly on my bike, I use the same standard.

Here is a list of my current pack items:

Constant items that don't change:

1. Compass
2. Map of the area
3. Magnifying glass
4. Signal mirror
5. Knife
6. A new cigarette lighter
7. A folding saw
8. Small duct tape roll
9. Twine
10. Binoculars
11. Two water bottles
12. Emergency hammer gel (a commercial energy gel in a long-lasting package)
13. A poncho in its organizing bag
14. A Gerber multi-tool I call a "girly man"
15. Cotton neck scarf for wearing wet in summer and for general use in winter
16. Radio (we use two-way radios when we go in a group)
17. An extra door key to my car
18. Contact lens case and solution
19. A small fuse box I use to put some pain pills in

20. My bike lights (two of them)
21. Fingernail clippers
22. Bear-sized pepper spray
23. An extra shirt
24. Jacket

Items that are seasonal:

For instance, I add this in winter:

1. Small propane stove
2. Two small aluminum cups
3. Tea bags, instant coffee & soups, hot chocolate packages
4. Rain pants
5. Gaiters
6. Neck gaiter
7. Two sets of gloves
8. OR-brand rain hat
9. North Face winter jacket

Items that are bike specific:

1. Small tire pump
2. Tool kit with allen wrenches, screwdrivers, and pliers
3. A spice jar filled with bolts, nuts, and small bike parts
4. A stuff-sack with extra parts for the bike, such as an extra sensor

Tracking-specific items:

1. Measuring stick
2. iPad for camera, field guide, and GPS mapping program that I can use offline
3. Pencils and notebook

Most of the time, especially when I am traveling on my bike, which is a mule that can carry a load, I use a thermos for coffee and leave the stove behind. By leaving it behind I mean it's in my car.

I keep a plastic storage tub in my car with things that are not in my pack that I might need. For instance, in summer, all the winter gear listed above is in my storage tub in the car. I might get somewhere with my summer gear and find I need that winter jacket, or I might want to unload my spring jacket and just take a long-sleeved shirt on really hot days. The tub in my car contains backup parts, different jackets, vests, and hats so that I can change out the things in my pack as conditions warrant. Also, if there were an emergency and I made it back to my car, I would be well-supplied.

My car also has a hidden key system so if I lose my keys, I have not lost the use of my car. I've known two friends who locked themselves out of their cars in a wilderness place, hours from home. In both cases, it involved a lot of nighttime driving to solve the crisis.

And think about this: What if you met some bad hombres trying to hassle you in various ways? What if they decided it would be fun to take your keys from you?

All I can say is keep a backup. More likely, however, is the big magnet in the earth that finds ways to suck your keys out of your pack and into a stream, a sinkhole, or a snowbank. Then of course there's the old "lock your keys in your truck" trick. Think about it ahead of time.

~ Stay Organized ~

Organization of your gear helps in every way. It's not enough to have a backpack with your gear in it. You need to be able to use that gear, find your snacks, and be able to replace things you take out. If all your gear goes in the same spot each time, it's really easy to see what's missing.

The same with your car. If you always put your extra water in the same spot, just a glance can tell you if you forgot it.

Sounds simple? Not really.

Backpacks are open spaces of weird shape that conform to your body. They don't have compartments and for certain, the thing you pack on the bottom is the first thing you are going to need. I have seen friends fail to use a piece of gear because it's in the bottom of their pack and too hard to get to. The results are never pretty.

For instance, you feel a hot spot forming in your boot, the very first signs of a blister. You keep walking, though, as the group you are with is in a hurry, or you're part of a rescue crew and your moleskin is in the bottom of your pack. Nope! Disaster about to happen!

What? You didn't even pack this blister cure?

Well, a cup of tea would help. Metaphorically speaking, though. I mean, stop and think about it for a minute. Just in case this actually happens to you, here is a trick: Flagging tape, which is unfortunately plentiful on most trails, can be wrapped around the sensitive part and it works to keep the spot from rubbing. It means you have to stop, sit down, take off your boot and sock, figure out how to wrap your foot, and then put it all back together again before you go on.

However, if you don't stop, you have committed yourself to one of the first mistakes that leads to others, and a good time gone very wrong.

There is no reason to be miserable.

Zero, zip, none.

~ Rescue Whom? ~

On one rescue mission I took part in, we had to walk up about two thousand feet of steep trail to even get to the area where they thought the subjects were stuck. I was in pretty good hiking condition at the time, but nevertheless, I had a pack full of everything I needed on my back.

After two o'clock that afternoon I started to fade. We had been working since about nine a.m., hiking uphill, crossing streams, and trying to hurry. We hadn't stopped. I started to get cranky. My team leader wasn't tired yet and kept on going.

Finally, after quietly suffering for a while, I spoke up and asked if we could stop for lunch.

My team leader wanted to get to the search area as soon as possible and said we'd stop as soon as we got there.

I looked at my map and realized we were probably another two hours away. Unfortunately, search and rescue team protocol doesn't allow you to split up from your team, or fall behind.

I'm afraid I lost my temper.

"Why in the hell do we carry all this gear if we aren't ever going to use it?"

I was allowed a quick bite, standing up, and some water. We didn't make it to the search area. The subjects who were stranded were picked up by a helicopter before we got up there.

Then we had the long, arduous task of rescuing ourselves. By the time I got back to my car, I was almost in need of the basket we put bodies in to carry them out.

And some people wonder why I love to go by myself!

It would have taken me an hour longer, at least, to reach the spot where we turned back. However, if I'd made it to where the subjects were stranded, I would have been in better shape to help and certainly in better shape to get back down the mountain.

The lessons learned that day, by our whole team, were important on every search we did after that.

Search and rescue organizations have what I believe to be the best possible training opportunities for their members. Most of the searchers are competent, well-trained individuals who volunteer their time and many hours of learning to help people. The money they invest in training and gear comes out of their own pockets. In our area at least, people are not required to pay for being rescued.

By all means, if there is a search group in your area, consider joining. The team becomes like family to each other, and the one thing no one tells you about being on a search group is that it's *fun.* Not only do you learn skills that no one else can help you with, there is something quite satisfying in helping people, even if they never know you were there.

Like all groups of people, though, you face the human elements of getting along, sort of like a rock band. Teams have their ups and downs.

Sometimes they get a group of people who are enthusiastically trying to be the best they can be and help each other to be good too, and sometimes there is an element who is not, and never will be, satisfied for whatever reason. The numbers of volunteers reflect these ups and downs.

If you can find a team that is on the way back from a down cycle, that would be a good time to join.

~ 22 ~

The Art of Observing

It starts with the wind. Every day the direction of the wind is going to be instrumental in a lot of things that will happen. By journaling my experiences every day, and entering the date, the time, and the weather, this started to make a lot of sense.

When I review my notes, my weather entries help me to age tracks and sign and patterns of activity. Because I make a habit of discerning the wind direction, the amount of cloud cover, the humidity, and the temperatures, when these things change it's much more noticeable. In this big picture of my surroundings, it's also helpful when I'm out in the wild to know what time the sun will set and when the crepuscular hours will turn to darkness. The phase of the moon means a lot to a wild animal. My tracking journal reflects this.

Because I make these things a daily habit, if I'm out in the back country and the wind stops, I notice. Then, I wait to see what direction it will blow from next. The sometimes subtle easement of wind means a change. A breeze in a new direction will change the way the smells waft around, the way the clouds move, and the humidity. Animals, who don't live in a house that isolates them from all these changes, are super sensitive to the slightest change. That's why I want to be alert to weather, too.

I used to focus on just animal sign in the woods because I was so fascinated to learn how the animals I don't see very often live and where they are. After thirty or so years of tracking, though, I've realized that tracking is easier if you look at the bigger picture. So now I want to know what the plants are, who is eating them or using them for nesting, and how they interact with all the other plants in the area.

I get really excited, for instance, to discover an oak tree that bears acorns hidden in a little wild valley. That's going to be food for a lot of animals. The rare wild apple tree and the dogwood trees are food vectors for birds and mammals. My sense of smell sometimes helps me find these treasures. I dearly wish I could smell as well as bears do, but with some practice I've started to be able to tell the difference between the smell of ripe huckleberries and salal berries.

Whenever I find a very obvious sign of animal passage, I have schooled myself to scrutinize the area around it as well. The last time I was in the woods, day before yesterday, Jane and I were planning on an exercise ride when she got stopped by some glaring (to us anyway) tracks on the dirt bank along the road. We stopped and parked the bikes to examine two bear tracks side by side and pushing up lots of dirt as the animal apparently jumped down the slope. Now why would a bear jump down a slope?

The area around these two tracks gave us lots of clues as we spent an hour and a half putting together more of the evidence. Several bears had been there not long before we came by. They pushed paths in and out of the roadside vegetation, scratched a log, broke some bark off, made what looked like a stomp trail of grinding the paws in to make holes in the forest duff, and lay down in the trickle of water from a spring on the hillside. As a whole, the evidence made me think of a couple of teenage bears, separated from their mother this year, but still hanging out and playing games.

It would have been easy to identify the two obvious tracks and simply move on. It was infinitely more entertaining to find the rest of the sign and picture the actions that had to have happened to make it.

The rewards of finding all the sign has made me a person who looks up and down the road, up in the trees, up the trail the animal came down, in the gravel, in the culverts, studies the plants and trees, and wanders slowly around to see, smell, and feel the energy of the place. While we looked, two ravens talked over our heads, and one flew by making the unmistakable sound of raven wings swishing. Two Douglas squirrels chased each other down a tree and sounded like a few deer as they raced through the vegetation and ran at full speed down the road towards us. They saw me about three feet from where I was watching them and screamed, then dove off the road in different directions.

When you find a spot like that, it's worth the time to observe and soak up as much information about the place as possible.

The more time I spend finding signs and tracks, the more I notice around me all the time. Spending time in Alaska as a bear-viewing guide, I learned that birds were particularly interested in what the bears were doing because they left scraps of food lying around. That prompted me to be interested in what the birds were saying. Wind on the lake moved the trees in a regular rhythm but a bear, scent-marking by rubbing on a tree, could be noticed across the lake by the way the tree moved. I still notice unusual tree and bush movements out of the corner of my eye.

Recently, watching a beaver pond with binoculars, I noticed unusual movement among the sedges, so I got to watch the disappearance of a whole leaf.

It's fun to know what the sound of a beaver eating is, or the sound of an elk grazing, ripping off the leaves of their preferred greenery.

My internal dialogue goes something like, "Oh, so that's what that looks like!" Or, "Now I know where that road comes out."

Each little thing that puts together the picture is stored in my bank of previous observations to be matched with new ones. Each one of them helps me answer the hundreds of questions every outing generates.

~ Look for the Cracks ~

After trying to find answers to the universe all my life, I've learned to look for the cracks. As humans, we seem to have such limited observation skills that we can totally convince ourselves of something that is just not true. Or we carry such a skewed version of truth that it's as useless as an ashtray on a motorcycle.

There are clues to the universe, though. Writers, artists, and musicians all talk about an experience of entities outside themselves contributing to their works in times when they are immersed in what they are doing and have forgotten about the "self." The other animals on the planet may have more access to what I like to call the cosmic order of things.

Observing with All Your Senses

Smelling the faint odors on the wind,

seeing the thousands of different colors of green,

feeling the texture of the dirt you're walking on,

hearing the croak of a raven and the swish of its wings

as it checks you out, and

tasting the sweet but woodsy burst of a huckleberry in your mouth—

these are all a start.

With practice, you can absorb more information than most people ever do. One of the "tricks" is not to put a name to things. Let the crack in your mind open and your sense of self disappear. Some people call this meditation and others call it a "quiet sit," but it works best if you can learn to do it like second nature, even when you're moving around.

When we're born into a body we become a self. There are many ways to talk about this and as many religions and beliefs as there are people. It's probably all wrong, even what I think about it is probably wrong. But I do still believe that there are keys we can find to get a sense of our insignificance, in one sense, and our importance in another. Immersing yourself into the study of the natural world provides some combinations to the locks.

On the beach one day, I interrupted a moon snail drilling a

hole with its router-style mouth into the end of a closed clam shell in order to suck out the animal and digest it. I saved the clam and deprived the moon snail of its meal. So, morally, which animal deserved any help from me? I eat meat and I eat clams, so why would I think I was an important enough Being to decide who lives and who dies in a tide pool? It absolutely makes no sense that I felt sorry for the clam. I became aware of the stupidity of my emotions.

Instead, I now try to learn what nature shows me without involving my ego and emotions.

I have seen this in other people; for example, as someone proudly tells me they don't eat anything with eyes—while I notice that the front of their jeep is plastered with dead yellow butterflies.

Then, on the other hand, we have humans who love to kill things just for kudos. Animals don't do this. They kill to eat or survive. Humans also kill unintentionally just by the way we live. We kill things every time we mow the lawn, or clear a piece of property to build a roadway or a bridge. And yet, of all the animals, we humans are the biggest bleeding hearts!

Becoming a student of the non-human world around us can help us with our inherent, deep-seated hypocrisy. The idea that animals are a "thing" that we own to do with as we please can be dismissed easily by anyone who has had a pet die.

Studying the life cycle of salmon, I was shocked to learn that a salmon will lay five thousand eggs or so, and maybe one or two of those eggs will become an adult salmon and return to the hatching area to carry on the species. The eggs and small fry of salmon feed all kinds of other animals, and the fingerlings who make it to the lake then eat millions upon millions of mosquito babies before they are scooped up by the thousands to feed other animals. Nature sacrifices all these babies for the good of the whole. So what happens to all the little souls and selves of these babies?

I'm sorry to make you think about this, but you'll be a better and far more interesting person if you do.

~ Grandmothers Know ~

When I was about ten years old, I visited my grandmother in her summer home in New Hampshire and was kicking around the house one day when I went into the kitchen to see her. She was making noodles and humming a song while she worked.

I said, "Grandma, I'm bored," and sat down at the kitchen table with a sigh.

She was quiet for a minute or two and then turned, with flour on her hands, and said, "Honey, I hate to break it to you, but you're not bored...you're boring."

I thought about that for a minute and got up to leave, but she softened the blow by adding, "I know it's hard to be away from your friends. But go outside and do something and you'll meet kids here."

I've been going outside to do something ever since.

Being out and about discovering things and observing does have a downside. I am no longer comfortable making small talk at a party or gathering, and I look for an escape as soon as I am in someone else's plan. I have a tendency to look out the window and plan my getaway unless someone wants to talk about things that are important to me, like finding ways to stop the animals from disappearing from Earth.

My own journey has become one where I realize that I know so very little about anything, and that each thing I discover—like that a certain bear eats hawkweed in June—just opens up many more questions. I don't have time for television, too much internet, or other pastimes that can't help my journey of discovery.

~ 23 ~

Guiding

Most of the time, guides get paid. However, after you learn the skills of a solo traveler and tracker, people will want to go with you and you'll want to take some of them. Learning to guide can also lead to a good job, especially if you work for a well-run outfit.

Guiding well is an art, though it's not an easy one. Not only do you need to fundamentally take care of yourself, you need to gently lead others into an adventure that they can handle, push them just a little out of their comfort, and bring them back excited and challenged and all in one piece.

If you're guiding professionally, you can shine if you understand that your group is ruled by your most inept, slowest guest. If you're walking up a steep trail, you're also going to have your macho or fit types at the front trying to set a pace and prove something. They will run over you, too, if they can.

I have been on both ends of this spectrum as a guest. But the one time I remember the most is when I was the last one on a multiple-day bike trip.

~ Last in Line, First in Importance ~

One mountain-climb day, I just couldn't keep up. When I pulled into the rest spot where the other bike guests where talking and resting in the shade I was hot, sweaty, and exhausted. They took my arrival as a sign that rest was over and got up and started to get ready to go.

The guide stood up and said, "Nope. The fifteen-minute rest starts now."

I got some dirty looks but I was able to recover and managed to keep up with the back of the pack from then on.

I learned a valuable guiding lesson on that trip. Had they moved on when I got there, I would have never been able to finish the day, as my exhaustion multiplied. I might have given up mentally and I certainly would have been mad as hell.

Your guests are delicate, like eggs. It's easy to crack them, but it's also easy to empower them to be better and stay involved. They come in all shapes and sizes, and from all kinds of preconceived notions and levels of expertise. Pulling a group together is not only important; it is the key to the success of any adventure.

~ Managing Expectations ~

It's important to realize that an adventure in which expectations are high will most likely disappoint.

When guests came to the bear-viewing lodge where I worked in Alaska, they had spent a bunch of money and done some adventurous traveling to get there. The first thing they would ask when they got off the floatplane was if they were going to see bears.

We learned not to pump them up with assurances. We'd say things like, "We hope so," and, "We'll try our best."

They wanted to know if we'd seen bears the day before.

We'd answer that, "Every day is different and there are many factors that determine if the bears are where we can see them."

These answers weren't the hype they read in the ads the booking agents used. In fact, several booking agents would guarantee bear sightings—which, of course, is impossible unless you go to a zoo. Most of our guests understood this.

Woe to the poor guide who told the folks that he saw seven or eight bears the day before and got to spend hours watching them. Boxing themselves in like that was a sure road to disappointed guests if the guide could only find one bear. Instead of appreciating the one bear, the guests were always going to compare what they got with what the people the day before got.

When you talk to a guest, don't look over their shoulder or down at them. Look at them levelly and in the eye. If you do this with every guest, no matter what, you won't have to spend as much time giving them personal attention. People who go on guided trips can't or don't want to do the trip themselves, but they also are not helpless or hopeless. (Usually, anyway.) Besides what you have to show them or share with them, they also have interesting lives and knowledge that you don't have.

The best guide I ever watched work was one of my fellow guides at the lodge in Alaska. He was such a confident and caring soul that he had a very fine sense of humor. No disgruntled guest ever experienced one of his trips without laughing and changing their minds about life. Since then, this has always been my standard. I believe the main skill he possessed that others lacked was his ability to pay absolute attention to where he was and the people with him.

We sometimes experienced days when the bears were absent. The best guides were able to make the trip worthwhile for their guests by giving them a good adventure anyway. For instance, walking on the floating bog with bare feet, stepping in the bear tracks and looking at carnivorous plants, or taking a hike to one of the small lakes along a bear trail and seeing other wildlife.

~ Monitoring Guests ~

When you travel by yourself, self-monitoring is an important part of keeping yourself safe. When you guide, you have to do the same thing but it is doubly hard because you have to monitor everybody else, too. You are responsible for the health, welfare, and mental attitude of the whole group. Not only professionally, but legally as well. Before you take a job guiding, find out what you can about the outfit and their insurance coverage, then be as observant as possible with your guests.

The miserable person in the back seat of the boat who won't look at anyone cannot be ignored. If you don't bring that person back, you can't bring your group together. As the guide, you need to discover whether it is a physical problem, like being cold or sick, or if there is a fear or personal relationship in your group that is creating the problem.

It was my habit to assume it was physical and offer solutions casually, such as handing them a blanket without asking if they need it. Or perhaps gently guiding them, without fuss, to a more secure place to sit. Their grateful response can open doors of inclusion and dialogue. You might look around and ask if anyone else needs a blanket.

Don't ever count on your "eggs" to tell you what's wrong. If they are miserable, they are usually past that. People just don't speak up. And unless it's a multi-day trip, you really don't know who that person is. It could be your boss's mother, for all you know.

Then you might encounter the problem of the insidious wrecker. The guest in the back who, as you're talking, leans over and whispers in someone's ear and they both chuckle. That is the guy (or gal) who doesn't respect you or what you are telling the group and isn't engaged. He (or she) will try to wrest the group from you from the back. There are a lot of successful ways to deal with this and they are all most effective if you do it right away. This person needs to be acknowledged and brought to the front of the action.

"Hey, Greg," you single them out, "you're taller than all of us, can you see if that bird nest has eggs in it?"

Sometimes you get a group that is already a unit and you, the guide, are the odd one out. The jokes are obscure and stay between them. They are having a good time, and then they turn on you for entertainment.

As a female boat captain, I grew well accustomed to this scenario. I got used to it to the point where I would agree with them that their lives were in grave danger with a "woman captain" and they'd better keep those life jackets on!

One time I hosted an executive who, I had been told, was a VIP of some kind. I was guiding the group on Big River Lake to watch bears feeding on the salmon streams. When I greeted the group at the boat, the boss asked me where my gun was.

I explained that we used pepper spray for protection in the unlikely event that a bear got out of hand.

He wasn't satisfied and made a show out of upbraiding me for unsafe practices.

I let him go on while I got the boat ready.

Then, just before he boarded, he wanted an answer to what I would do if the little can of pepper spray didn't work.

Silently, I unlatched the fire extinguisher and pulled the pin and aimed it in his direction.

To his credit he put up his hands and laughed. The group boarded the boat and things got off to a better start.

Later in the day, when it looked like the bears were all asleep somewhere and they weren't going to get to see any, the group started to get restless. They were giving me stink eye like it was my fault.

My friend Susan James, who had the other half of their group on another boat near me, was getting the same treatment from her group. They started to fume about "women captains."

Susan and I needed to change the vibe, not just for the group, but for the bears. These guys were all pacing on the boat and staring into the woods like tigers in a cage looking for the steak. The bears, who were watching from under cover, probably thought they looked like predators.

When we talked on the radio quietly, Susan suggested, since it was a nice warm day, that the guys all take off their shoes. That was met with disbelief, then disgust, then humor, and finally, they all did it.

As soon as they sat down and started looking at the holes in each other's socks and white bare feet, they all relaxed and turned their attention elsewhere. They laughed and joked.

Having bare feet in the Alaska wilderness is such a foreign thought to most that it completely changed their energy. The bears no longer felt threatened and came out of the woods to fish.

This was a case of thinking outside the box and getting the group to do something they could do, but that they would never think of. They had a great day. Not one of them was unhappy when they left.

~ You First ~

I've certainly had my failures as a guide. I have had people try to run over me and sometimes be successful enough to cut the class or trip short. My failures all have one thing in common: I was personally uncomfortable for some reason.

Once, it was 100 degrees and I was trying to teach a class. Another time it was raining and cold and I was getting hypothermic. Both times I lost the patience needed to deal with others.

That is why the first thing you need to learn in order to be a good guide is how to take care of yourself. Because if you don't, and try to push through, you could hurt someone—or at the very least, ruin everyone's day. Your observations need to be sharp and not turned inward. Staying comfortable and relaxed makes you funny and fun to be with.

~ It's Not What You Know ~

The knowledge of the natural world that a guide needs is unending. No way can a person learn everything about the natural world in one lifetime. There is always a tree or a spider or bird you don't know the name of, but that doesn't matter. It's not what you know or don't that makes you a good guide. Instead, it's your way of being, and your way of discovering, that you need to share.

I've learned, especially as I teach tracking, that simply giving people the name for something is lame and ineffective. No one remembers something they don't have to work for.

Say, you and a group come upon a nice line of bear tracks on a dusty road. Everyone wants you to say what it is right away.

But if you do that, all the rest of the discoveries are lost.

If you say, "Oh look, bear tracks," the group wants to move on, as they have learned all they think they can learn. Nope.

What about the size of the tracks, the measure of the stride, and then what gait the animal is moving in and what the animal is seeing, smelling, and feeling from where it made the tracks?

What about the tracks that the animal made coming in to the spot, and the ones it made leaving?

What about the trail it used to get off the road, and where it came from?

Which paw is which, and why, and what exactly makes it unmistakably a bear track?

If a bear was there, then what was it doing, and where is it now?

The group can go even deeper with a few tracks if they look for things that make that animal unique, such as a broken claw, or a small rock showing between the digits. Where the bear turned its head or hesitated. You may find a whole, long story on the ground. But unless you know to look for it, you won't see it.

That's where a guide helps by asking the right questions and getting people to slow down and really look and discover. A good guide makes people think and make discoveries themselves. That is the value of the adventure, and the unforgettable part.

~ Keep Them Looking ~

Yesterday my friend Jane and I were driving a back road headed to a bike ride when I spotted something big and black in the road. I thought it was a tire piece and called her on the radio. (We take two cars for safety and use radios to keep in touch.) She was driving behind me.

"Hey, was that scat?"

"Indeed it is," she answered.

We pulled over to find a pile of hair and bones wrapped in unspeakable dead meat, delicately placed in the middle of the road in what looked like pee. We measured and photographed and looked around.

We found several fresh trails off the road that were as wide as bears. It looked like one of the berry-eating bears Jane and I had been following got into the carcass of an ungulate. When we took our time, we noticed that there were drops of water on the pavement as well, probably as the bear approached the spot where it left the scat. The weeds and vegetation in the area were still quite wet with dew, and we figured the bear was dripping. Because the drops were drying before our eyes, we knew we had just missed the bear.

When we looked a little further, we found the ribs of a bloody deer carcass pulled up on the edge of the road. Tire tracks led us to believe a hunter had pushed the remains of a carcass off the road there. The bear, indeed, had been helping clean up the mess.

It would have been easy to stop looking for clues after we discovered the water drops on the road.

When you are guiding, it is important to know when to move on and when you can get more of an experience out of an animal sighting or track event. The impulse is to move on, but excitement isn't around every corner in the wild. When you find some, make sure you explore and evaluate it to its fullest.

~ Thrive in Your Outdoor Jobs ~

Besides guiding, there are many other jobs that require outdoor skills. Research groups, Forest Service personnel, monitoring data, and trail work are just a few of the things you can get paid for.

One researcher I know tells me that when he needs to hire someone for working in the wild, studying animals, he looks for a person who is capable of doing field work. That's someone who knows how to get a truck unstuck, change a tire, hike forbidding terrain, and remain thoughtful and calm. That person doesn't need to call for help, and has enough savvy to help others. He'd take a competent person over a degree any day. He also looks for kind, caring people. Personalities that lighten the load, not make it harder on everyone.

That makes sense to me.

However, as a woman who probably can't change a truck tire by myself, I would be careful and just wouldn't get a flat or blow out a tire in the first place. I'd give the truck with the sketchy tires to the guys. I also wouldn't get the truck stuck. I always walk sketchy sections first and then make a plan. And I've been laughed at for that, but knock on wood, I've only gotten stuck in the snow once and I figured out how to get myself out. After all, anyone can be strong if we just use the biggest muscle we have, which is the one between your ears.

When I was a yacht captain responsible for hiring crew, it didn't matter what the person's gender was as long as they had common sense and the imagination to find solutions to problems. Most of the time you live with crew on a boat, at least for some time, and I could tell right away if someone was going to last merely by how they organized their personal gear. If you looked in an engineer's cabin, for instance, and the bed was unmade and dirty clothes covered the floor, chances were pretty good that things would start going wrong elsewhere on the boat.

There are reasons to be organized and methodical in your approach to working outdoors. You'll have enough to deal with—other people, weather, events you can't predict, and the potential success of your venture. That's why I organize my car, my pack, and my gear at home so that each item goes back in the same place each time. That way I can tell at a glance if something is missing, or put my hand on a needed tool without searching for it.

I've had to fire a few guides and crew over the years. I'd say the biggest mistake an adult can make is to ask the question, "But what about me?" That tells me that the person hasn't learned how to take care of themselves. They need someone else to do it, and it means they won't be able to care for guests either.

Another one I had to let go was the new engineer on the

vessel I was running who came to the bridge to tell me, "You have a problem with one of the starboard generators."

Inserting the "you" instead of "we" was all I needed to understand his attitude. I think I gave him the benefit of the doubt for a few days in case it was a slip of the tongue, but he proved to be a backseat boss who tried to turn the crew against me. That's a problem you can't fix and can't live with. He didn't last a week.

If your outdoor skills are your bread and butter, keep working on those skills. Not only do you need the competence to take care of yourself and foresee problems, but you need to be able to work with people. If you're the boss, don't let problems slide. Fix them right away, either by firing or ironing it out, because a bad crew member is like a bad tooth. They'll only get worse if neglected.

Working outdoors can be incredibly rewarding in many ways, but making money usually isn't one of them. For some reason, owners and managers feel that working outside is a reward in itself, and salary and benefits don't need to be big to attract workers. They're right, of course, so in order to work outside you need to plan your life accordingly. It helps if your life expenses are very low to start with. It also helps if the outfit you work for provides room and board. The other secret to making it work is not to spend much.

I used to watch in amazement as my Alaska boat crew would spend an entire paycheck at the bar between trips. Drinks for everybody...then in a week they would ask for an advance.

There are lots of ways to make your outdoor skills provide you with a living, but be careful that you don't lose the personal joy of the wild. Working at what you love can ruin your enjoyment of it, unless you think about it ahead of time and plan your time. Becoming a fishing guide, for instance, can ruin fishing for you—after taking off the thousandth ruined fish for a client and watching them frenzy into catching more than they need. Pick your jobs carefully and use your time off to take care of yourself.

~ 24 ~

Reaching Out to Young People

I once tried to teach tracking to kids, back when I taught classes for the county recreation department where I live. I must admit that I didn't know how. I realized my deficiency in teaching youngsters one day when my class joined me at a Forest Service campground.

Before they got there, I found really cool bear tracks in a natural spring.

After the class was settled, I led them to the spring to point out the mother bear's tracks and the little tracks of her two cubs. I was pretty excited by the find, and I mistakenly thought they would be too.

They were bored.

I had them sit in the grass nearby so I could tell them more about bears and their lives. As soon as I started talking one kid raised a hand.

I said, "Yes?"

"Ms. Hunter, we saw a deer in our yard."

"That's cool. What was it doing?"

"I don't know."

"Did you watch it?"

"No."

End of conversation.

Back to bears. Another hand went up.

"What time is lunch?"

Somehow I got through that class without hurting anyone.

I realized much later, while guiding in Alaska and tracking for a whole lot more years, that there is a way to teach kids about the outdoors.

Some wonderful trackers have addressed this. Jon Young's book, *Coyote's Guide to Connecting with Nature,* is a must for teachers and parents. Jon realized that mentoring was a skill that trackers need in order to teach.

You can only show, not tell, and you need to get kids involved in hands-on adventures. You need to have them crawling in the grass, or getting intimately involved with mud. Or you should wear them down with a big hike before you let them discover the cool things there are to see.

It's really rewarding to see the look of wonder on a kid's face when they first see salamander eggs floating in their jelly casing in a pond. The secret is to have them discover it.

I have influenced more young people by just being me than I have trying to get them to notice and realize things.

But I like to teach adults and leave the kids to others who are good at it. My theory is that I can teach adults who will take the knowledge and pass it on to their kids and grandkids.

When I was young, outdoor education was more like, "You kids turn off the TV and go outside and play!"

Unfortunately, we can't do that everywhere now, so educational opportunities like Treesong Nature Awareness and Retreat Center are what kids need. This non-profit has held outdoor classes for years for home-schooled kids, as well as classes for kids of all ages in Portland, Oregon, and Vancouver, Washington.

Every year I do a campfire program for Oxbow Park, a Portland Metro Park. The campers in the area are mostly families with kids. It's usually getting dark, near bedtime, with a cheery fire burning in an outdoor setting. Before the audience arrives, I sneak a full-size cardboard grizzly bear into the brush behind me, where the light just barely catches it. It takes the audience a while to notice it and, after dark, it looks real.

Then all I need to do is tell them bear stories! I can do that:

When I was a little girl, about your size (I point to a girl in the audience who is squirming), I went camping with my family in a campground much like this one.

The ranger told us there were animals around and to keep our food secure because we could attract bears or other animals that would eat our food.

My Dad set up the tents while my Mom cooked up some hot dogs and put potato chips and macaroni salad on our plates. When we were finished, my Dad carefully burned the paper things, wiped out the other things, and took them to the secure trash cans.

It was time for bed. I got put with my two brothers—who were about your size (I point to a couple of brothers wrestling in the back)— in a pup tent with three sleeping bags in it, and my baby sister went in the tent with Mom and Dad. After we turned out the flashlights and snuggled in, it was really dark.

My older brother said, "I wonder if bears will eat us, since we didn't leave any food out for them?"

My younger brother said, "Bears don't eat people, do they?"

"Yup, they sure do."

My older brother was quite sure of this.

Billy, my younger brother, said, "I'm scared."

My Dad said from the other tent, "Quiet down now and go to sleep."

We stopped talking and started whispering about bears and wild animals and how much protection a tent is…or isn't.

Finally we stopped and Billy fell asleep. My older brother, Mike, fell asleep too. But I didn't.

I was listening to everything and felt that, since my whole family was asleep, I needed to stay awake. It wasn't long until my heart was pounding in response to a loud cracking noise, seemingly just outside the tent.

I woke up my brothers and we all three listened to a grinding, gnawing sound, along with wood splintering and snuffling.

"We'd better wake up Dad," I said.

My older brother Mike called out. It took a few times before my Dad answered gruffly.

Of course, the noise stopped when my brother called out, so Dad wasn't too happy with us.

But both our parents must've been lying awake after that, because when the noise started up again we heard my Mom say, "Steve, what is that?"

We heard a murmuring reply. Finally, with a big sigh, my dad started getting dressed and we heard him unzip the tent. As we peeked out, he turned on the flashlight and played it around the area. There didn't seem to be anything there. My Dad stood still until the noise started up again and then he strode off.

I ducked my head under the sleeping bag 'cause I just knew

he was going to find a bear.

We heard him walking, then a muffled oath drifted our way. Then we heard a board being ripped off something and go crashing into the brush.

Wow, I thought, my Dad just hit a bear with a board!

When he came back, he ducked down into the opening of our tent and told us it was just porcupines eating the back of the outhouse. He said he ripped off the board they were chewing on and threw it down the slope. The porcupines gave him a dirty look and then waddled down the hill to finish the job.

Kids need stories and they need to be wild outdoors. We used to get to play hide and seek. At night, the whole neighborhood of kids at the lake cottage would go out and play Kick the Can, using all our stealth skills and night vision. Camping was amazing, especially if we were next to a beach where kids could run wild.

What kids don't do well with is quiet time in nature, and slowing down to nature time. But they benefit if they are around adults who practice that.

Mentoring a child after learning about the wild can be very rewarding. One of the ways to do this very effectively is to use your storytelling skills. One of the best ways for little ones to learn about nature is through stories read or told aloud, with animation and feeling.

My first introduction to the Native American tradition of call-and-response storytelling was in one of Jim Halfpenny's tracking classes in Yellowstone. Among the class members was master storyteller Jim Bruchac, of Abenaki descent, who told an animal story using the "Hey/Ho" method. The storyteller adds a "Hey" and the audience responds with "Ho." It's a good way to thoroughly engage a young audience.

As a naturalist, you can get involved in all kinds of programs, for kids of all ages and economic levels. If you are interested in passing on your outdoor adventures, look into some local programs and sign up.

In the long run, influencing kids to "be wild" will help us protect the earth.

~ 25 ~

Returning to Earth

One day you may discover that you can no longer sink easily to your knees to look at tracks or sign, then easily rise back up. That's the bad news. The good news is that you can learn to do things in new ways and keep going.

The inevitable thing about being alive is that we get older. The process is not a linear one, however. We all have years of poor health and recovery, and even better health is sometimes possible as you age. Changes in situation, diet, and lifestyle can make a person stronger.

The most important part is to keep moving however you can. Almost everything, physically and mentally, can get better if you keep the blood moving. The body is a machine and you don't want your parts to get rusty.

The last time I rode Cycle Oregon, a multi-day bike tour of Oregon, a guy with long white hair passed by me every day yelling, "On your left!" One lunch stop I talked to him. He was eighty-six. I asked his advice about getting older. He simply said, "Move it or lose it"—a sentiment I keep in mind all the time.

It's interesting how your ideas about health and death can change as you get closer to nature. Watching how Mother Nature structures life can teach you how to live your own life.

Watching wild animals go through their lives gives us inspiration about death and the beautiful, natural order of procreation and termination. The more we absorb about the earth (where people have not altered nature into nonexistence), the more comfortable we are with life and death.

Most human beings follow some kind of religion because it's a very basic part of our make up to fear death. "Survival instinct" is a cliché used to describe this desperation to live at all other costs. However, organized religion is fraught with human ego and our manipulative tendencies. It's too easy to use this primal fear to make people behave in certain ways. I'll just leave it at that, as there are many other books that explore this phenomenon at length.

All earthly forms of animals, plants, bugs, fungi, and living organisms have a code they live by, created by the energy and circumstances of their survival. They have feelings and emotions which they share, if you know how to look for them.

They also use subterfuge; such as bears who pretend they don't see you, opossums who "faint" when they get scared, insects who have what look like eyes on their backs, and camouflage of all types. Who knows? Ant colonies might even use cults and propaganda to keep their members in line.

All of which underlines how much we resemble our fellow animals. A person can spend a lifetime contemplating the meaning of life and death, but as long as we are trapped in earthly bodies, we can only know very little.

If you accept that we are but a small part of a bigger river of life, you can see more clearly into the world of nature. The part of you that is ego can be strongly attached to your body, in which case, you'd believe that death is final and afterlife is nonexistent. If, on the other hand, you've watched a pack of wolves kill an elk, you might have noticed that at some point the fight for survival ends with acceptance on the part of the elk.

We all came from somewhere before we were born and we're all headed for somewhere when we die. Nature doesn't value being alive as much as we do. Otherwise, five thousand viable salmon eggs born from one mother wouldn't transform into fingerlings with only a very few of them destined to survive. Every bird egg cannot survive or they would wipe out the bugs, and every fawn born doesn't become an adult because the earth's flora couldn't handle that many ungulates.

Nature ruthlessly controls populations of all kinds of living things to balance a habitat. The river of life ebbs and flows, and tides come and go. Years of nature observation and animal studies can make you feel a whole lot easier about the big picture of life.

I am fond of saying that all ships are sinking, some faster than others. In your life, you will ebb and flow, and maybe when you can no longer hike ten miles a day, you will set up a blind with a camera and serve as your own trail camera. You could even do that in a wheelchair. Which brings me to the subject of older or disabled trackers.

During one of the CyberTracker evaluations in which I participated, I had learned enough about my older self to have the foresight to bring my small aluminum camp chair. After giving my answers for a group of questions, I was able to sit while waiting for everyone to finish. At lunch I didn't have to sit on the ground and I was able to stave off exhaustion and diminishing mental powers a bit longer. In looking over my evaluation scores over the years, I see a pattern based on my comfort level at each different weekend. My best scores so far were when the weather was good and I was in good shape for walking.

There are differing opinions among the tracking community about physical capabilities. Some say that physical abilities should be part of becoming a certified tracker. Rightfully, if you plan to work in research and the science fields, or law enforcement, or search and rescue, you need to be fit and strong, with a deep knowledge of the subject matter. On the other hand, there are avid outdoor people who are no longer going to be doing long miles or steep terrain. Many of them use their knowledge for photography, art, and, just like in native cultures, these people often become teachers and storytellers.

If part of your work is trailing animals, you know that they already possess superior four-wheel drive with their four legs, and the ability to navigate very challenging terrain. The bears I've trailed have been able to flummox me sometimes, not because I couldn't see their trail, but because I couldn't physically go where they went. Still, I've been able to piece together the knowledge of several bears' lives, even if I can't walk their trails through the swamps and vegetation tunnels.

Jane and I had been tracking a bear for weeks. I already knew a lot about him, including that it was a male from the size of his tracks, scat, stomp trail, bite marks, fur left behind, day beds, browse signs showing what he was eating, and the age of the tracks he left. After I sat silently on my camp chair in a nearby meadow for a while, sketching by myself, that bear must have forgotten I was there. Or he decided that I wasn't going to move. For whatever reason, he came up out of his steep, tangled woodland to browse. Watching him graze along a fence line where he'd left frequent tracks confirmed everything I'd learned about him from his spoor. If I were younger, without arthritis, I might have trailed him to his woodland retreats. Instead, I knew to wait for him in a place he frequently visits.

As we age, we learn to deal with new issues as they come up. Old injuries, diseases, and just plain gravity still exist, but it's my personal intention to deteriorate as slowly as possible.

Becoming a tracker, naturalist, birder, or all-round avid observer gives you strong motivation for adjusting to new physical limitations in order to keep going.

As you age, pay more attention to your gear. Some other things you might consider include:

A good pair of binoculars with a close-focus feature. "Close focus" means you can see things on the ground up close from a standing position, things that you once knelt to see.

Good binoculars can also allow you to see sign up a steep slope you once might have scrambled up without a thought of how you were going to get down again.

A sturdy pair of walking sticks can ease knees and keep you from falling.

Yoga classes, morning stretches, more walking, climbing stairs, and eating more vegetables definitely helps.

When you visit your eye doctor, don't be shy about telling her/him that you spend a great deal of time in the natural world, observing. Your eyes can be adjusted by glasses and contacts for different focal points. (In my experience, eye doctors just assume from my gender and age that I will be doing mostly indoor and up-close work. Over the years, I have wasted at least two human tracking classes with the wrong prescription of contact lenses. Even after explaining what I wanted, two different optometrists couldn't wrap their heads around a middle-aged woman tracking humans and animals in the woods!)

Fortunately, hearing aids have come a long way, and when you start to miss hearing bird language that you know should be audible, don't wait to start correcting this sense. It's important not to miss that subtle "huff" of a mother bear communicating with her cub, or the sound of a hummingbird coming to see if you're sweet.

Your sense of touch and smell are two senses that can be exercised in order to keep them strong. Learning to become aware of a slight breeze that changes direction and wafts the faint smell of carrion your way might help you discover new signs.

Consciously monitoring your abilities in each of the physical senses can indicate which things you need to spend more time on. You might have to use different ways of observing as you age, but you can figure it out. That drive and passion to learn more is a huge motivation for finding your own way.

Both the United States and Canada feature miles of designated, wheelchair-friendly trails. You'll find many organizations and resources dedicated to getting all people out into the wild. First comes your desire, then your research, and then you're unstoppable. Just because you can no longer bushwhack off trail doesn't mean you can't experience meaningful adventures!

I am lucky that so far both my hearing and smelling abilities haven't diminished. Twenty years from now, if you see an old lady out in the wilderness by herself studying bugs, birds, weeds, and seeds with a pet skunk hanging about, that'll be me.

And I'll probably tell you a story.

~ 27 ~
Magic

When you've learned to see tracks and sign in the wild, you can't unlearn it. As a result, you can be walking down a trail and glance to the side and see a clear bear trail in the weeds and duff. No one with you can see it, because they haven't put in the time you have. If you mention it, they'll think you're daft...or at least that you have happened upon some magical thinking.

If you recall, there once was a time when you couldn't see trails and tracks everywhere around you.

Logic should tell us all that there's more to learn. One of the magical things about nature is how complex, intense, and fascinating the whole construction of the earth and animals is. We could never learn it all. There are stories in the way trees grow, the way plants use some areas and not others. Lately, people are discovering that trees communicate and fungi are a part of their network. Each species of animals is complicated and amazing. Which is why we keep going back to learn new things. We want to know. We keep searching for the true stories of nature.

Asking questions about what we see is part of it. Discovering the answers takes time. Evidence that is discernible, unique, and right in front of your eyes can be translated into fact, using logic. Although magical thinking may come up with theories about cause and effect, the tracker wants hard evidence.

I was once asked by a lawyer, who was defending a person who had been in a crash where the other driver died, to look at an accident site. The relatives were trying to prove it was the living driver's fault. The attorney asked me to look at the crash site with fresh eyes and didn't tell me anything about the accident.

What I saw was a sloped curve where the two cars hit. The accident had happened on a cold and snowy night. It was spring when I looked at the sign. Along one side of the road you could see where a vehicle, a small pickup by my estimation, had gone off the road and sputtered alongside, slipping, and finally came back on the road, pushing down and breaking one of those plastic reflector posts. I pointed out to the lawyer what I saw, and why.

In a very short time a State Trooper was in my face yelling at me that I hadn't been to the accident scene (he had) and that the snow and ice were gone and that I knew nothing and was completely wrong. They told me that the living driver had gone off the road heading east, and was out of control and came back on the road and hit the other car.

I listened, but I wouldn't back down on what I saw. Pretty soon a state traffic inspector came to reason with me. He told me that the car tracks I was seeing were eastbound, not westbound. I listened and then I asked one question. Why, then, was the plastic road marker broken and pushed to the west?

His answer was that it was cold and frozen and probably bent over to the east and then whipped back to the west and broke.

I really tried to keep a straight face when he told me this. They were all mad at me because I had completely negated their accident report.

I was tired of all these guys yelling at me, so I asked to go home. I wished the lawyer good luck and tried to forget about a grown man who was supposed to be an expert insisting that a plastic marker could do that.

It must have been at least four months later when the attorney called me to apologize for putting me through that. A high school kid had come forward and said he was first to the accident scene and freaked out, drove off the road in his little pickup truck, drove around the accident going west, broke the plastic marker, and sped home to get someone to call the police. He was embarrassed that he hadn't stopped to see if he could help, so he kept quiet for a long time.

~ The Book of Tracking Bulls**t ~

In "The Book of Tracking Bulls**t" (as seasoned trackers call this phenomenon) things manage to do magic. Plastic markers suffer whiplash, people walk backwards for miles, and animals can appear around American chicken coops, even if they only live in India. Questioning information from others is part of a tracker's skill. Getting the full story is important.

I used to tell guests on my boat in Alaska that grizzly/brown bears didn't climb trees. As a matter of fact, one day I was repeating something I'd read about the difference in the length of claws that allow black bears to climb and keeps brown bears on the ground.

I was facing my passengers while right behind me there

was a brown bear who must have heard me, because she went right up a tree near shore and her two cubs followed her up.

I had passed on information I'd read. After I turned and saw the bear we called Mona up the tree with her cubs, my face turned red. But we all got a good laugh out of it. I couldn't figure out any other reason for Mona to have gone up that tree, except the leer on her face as they all swung in the breeze.

Not all guides or teachers are saints, though. Sometimes tracking bulls**t is just too tempting. Harvester ants, for instance, move house once in a while and leave a trail that is wide and clear to see. It looks like a snake track. A really big snake. How fun to see the frightened face of a new tracker when they try to picture this snake. Until a savvy student asks what gait the snake is using because they can't see the earth pushes a snake makes.

The Clif Bar trick also makes the Book. Instructors take a Clif Bar out of the package and roll it up to look like scat. They place it on a handy rock, and when students come around, they exclaim that it is rare, or a cougar scat. They pick it up and smell it and then lick it. When the students look especially uncomfortable, they take a bite and declare it delicious.

Then there are things that sound like bullsh*t but only because you're with someone who has different mental images than you and can see what you can't. One of my favorite trackers, Terry Kem, used to get me all the time because he could look in a mud puddle and see the marks of moth wings or tiny vole tracks. From him I learned that when you glance around and don't see anything, it means you look again. Terry can find small tracks better than anyone I know.

When I was a new student at Universal Tracking Services,

at a weekend class for human trackers from law enforcement and search and rescue, I mentioned to one instructor that I had read Tom Brown's books. I never met Tom Brown, a famous tracker from the East Coast. But when I mentioned his name in the law enforcement environment, you'd think I just pulled a pet skunk out of my pocket. Everyone moved away from me.

Finally, one of the instructors told me that Mr. Brown showed up at a search in Native American regalia and "proceeded to take over, claiming that he was an expert tracker." Then something happened that was bad. They weren't specific but insinuated that people like Tom Brown "just can't be tolerated" in a serious environment.

Tom Brown can see pressure releases and has studied them for years. Pressure releases are characteristics in tracks that show movement, intent, and details about the person or animal making the tracks. Details that are sometimes hard to believe. Which is why many law enforcement personnel are way skeptical when you tell them the person of interest weighs two hundred pounds and is wearing a backpack. If they can't see it too, it's not true, and you are loony.

The wise tracker sticks to what you can show someone else as a fact.

Like, "Here is my footprint in this substrate and here is the subject's. I weigh one-fifty and my track sank in this far. Right next to it is the subject's track and it's in the sand a bit further."

And about the backpack, "Here's a spot on the trail where he set it down." You can point out the wrinkle marks of the material. And yes, "he," as his trail is turned out too much to be female and, besides, here is where he stood and over there is where his pee landed."

~ True "Magic" ~

Then there is the true magic of nature that we are learning about so slowly.

Who knew that trees talk to each other? Who knew that fungus had such an important role to play in a habitat? For a long time, people thought cougars and bears were solitary animals. (And that grizzlies don't climb trees.)

Because animals don't have a language like humans, but rather have other means of communicating, we don't understand their worlds. One of the important things for nature to teach us is that we just don't know it all. Nor will a whole lifetime of observing with fascination give us all the answers. The willingness to say to ourselves we don't know it all, and may not find out, is the mark of a true student of nature.

For instance, animals seem to know more about death than we do. They may have cosmic connections with the universe that we can't even imagine. Aldo Leopold's words about shooting a wolf and then watching as the "green fire" in the wolf's eyes faded until she died have haunted outdoor enthusiasts ever since. What is that all about?

Some species have thousands of babies and only a few become adults and grow to procreate. Several mammals have the built-in birth control called delayed implantation. Trees can send first aid to their neighbors. Opossum mothers sometimes eat their young, and many other species used varied mechanisms to regulate their progeny in order for the species to survive. There are miracles all around us.

And yet we humans think we are special, not even part of

the animal world, civilized way beyond wild animals. I guess the human race is due a comeuppance, as all empirical evidence points to what we call magic, or things we don't understand. After all, things in the universe do what they do, and we don't get to "manage" it.

When you are lying on your back tonight, watching the stars and feeling the earth turn under your body, hopefully you will feel small and full of wonder. We're all on a wild ride and none of us know where it will go. All we can do is tap into the magic, enjoy the wonder, learn as much as we can, and be flexible in our knowledge.

Tomorrow, when you are pausing in the woods to see if you can hear trees talk, take a deep breath, and realize that if you just relax, the world will take you where you need to go.

Keep on tracking and making your own good tracks in life.

NATURE STUDY RESOURCES

Every person is the center of their own relationship with the world. Therefore, my list of resources will resemble a pebble thrown into a pond, with me at the center. The resources will be like ripples moving out from me in every direction. Therefore, in this list you won't find all the cool stuff out there about the outdoors and tracking, but you will find some of my personal favorites. Hopefully that will start you on making your own ripples in the pond.

I'll take a second here to apologize to all the authors, teachers, outdoor schools, and tracking resources that I must leave out because I haven't personally experienced them. Also, I have listed these resources and people in a random manner, so don't read anything into the order in which I present them.

~ Visual Animal Trackers ~

Dr. Mark Elbroch

My go-to book for anything I can't understand in the wild is Mark Elbroch's (with Casey McFarland) ***Mammal Tracks & Sign: A Guide to North American Species.*** It is a big paperback field guide. I don't carry it with me, but it is close to my desk for frequent reference.

All of the books that Mark Elbroch has been involved with are important and worth putting into your natural history library. Here are a few of them:

Field Guide to Animal Tracks and Scat of California by Mark Elbroch, Michael Kresky, Jonah Evans

Animal Skulls: A Guide to North American Species by Mark Elbroch

Bird Tracks & Sign: A Guide to North American Species by Mark Elbroch, Eleanor Marks

Peterson Reference Guide To The Behavior of North American Mammals by Mark Elbroch, Kurt Rinehart (A very useful guide to complement the track and field guides, especially if you want to know what the animals look like and how they survive.)

Jon Young

This author and tracker has made a huge impact on the way people see the natural world. Here are three of his essential books. If you look into his journey as a tracker, you will find a treasure trove of information and life experiences.

Animal Tracking Basics by Tiffany Morgan, Jon Young (I refer to this book often, always gleaning new insights.)

What the Robin Knows: How Birds Reveal the Secrets of the Natural World by Jon Young

Coyote's Guide to Connecting with Nature by Jon Young, Ellen Haas, Evan McGown, Richard Louv

Kim Cabrera

This influential tracker can be found on several Pages on Facebook where her goal is to educate new trackers and add to the knowledge of others. She is a marvel at educational videos. You can find her work at **bear-tracker.com** where she offers a pretty complete list of links to online tracking sites. On Facebook she maintains a presence in the "Animals Don't Cover Their Tracks: Animal Track Identification Help Group"and the "CyberTracker Specialist Evaluation Study Buddies"

Facebook groups. Most interesting though, are her YouTube "Beartracker Nature Films," incredible films depicting animal behavior and sign.

Louis Liebenberg

A man who has made a long-lasting impact on the way we preserve the art of tracking in the modern world. ***Practical Tracking: A Guide to Following Footprints and Finding Animals*** by Louis Liebenberg, Adriaan Louw, and Mark Elbroch, is a book you need in your library.

Lee Gutteridge
Kersey Lawrence

Not necessarily in that order; I couldn't decide which one of them to put first but they both are part of Original Wisdom, a company that teaches in South Africa, as well as in the U.S. You can find them at **originalwisdom.com**. Take a look at the calendar on their website to get an idea of the scope of wisdom these two trackers share about the natural world. I've had the honor of tracking with them both, and the thought that comes to mind is that *attitude is everything*. A treat.

Dr. James Halfpenny

I was fortunate to get an introduction to Yellowstone National Park by participating in one of Halfpenny's classes. We saw bears, wolves, elk, birds, and lots of interesting and wonderful tracks. Dr. Halfpenny has written and published an entire nature library. His extensive work in the wild is priceless. You can access his work at the bookstore on his website, **tracknature.com**.

Paul Rezendez

Tracking & the Art of Seeing by Paul Rezendes jumped off the shelves into my hands early on in my tracking journey. Easily digestible information about a wide range of animals graces the pages. The book is still on my desk, though admittedly some of the information is dated now, as the many avid trackers who came along later added a bunch of information to the pool of knowledge. It's still a good book to start with.

CyberTracker

Weird name, right? Yet this is one of the biggest organizations for tracking worldwide. It all started when tracking guides in Africa, specifically Louis Liebenberg, wondered if there was a way to get tracking data out of the native guides who knew so much about animals yet spoke different languages. They developed computer technology to make a symbols-based interface through which trackers could record data by pressing on pictures. I owned one of the first prototypes for a while and it was a genius solution. Since then, the CyberTracker organization has grown into a worldwide certification program that tests trackers. Find them at **trackercertification.com**. While you are there, look up the evaluators and you'll find a group of people who have more resources for your education than I can list here.

David Moskowitz

Wolves in the Land of Salmon is one of my favorite Moskowitz books, as well as ***Wildlife of the Pacific Northwest: Tracking and Identifying Mammals, Birds, Reptiles, Amphibians and Invertebrates,*** and ***Caribou Rainforest: From Heartbreak to Hope.*** David is somewhat elusive as he's always out in the field, but if you catch up with him in a class or evaluation, his knowledge is deep and ever increasing.

Pinau Merlin

A Field Guide to Desert Holes by Pinau Merlin is a must guide for desert tracking. It's a small book, easily tucked into a pack, but full of natural history.

Charley Eiseman
Noah Charney

Tracks and Sign of Insects and Other Invertebrates: A Guide to North American Species is a guide I take with me to Baja, Mexico, every year. You can never learn enough about bugs and their relationships to other animals and plants. This volume can solve many a mysterious finding in the woods or sand dunes.

Filip Tkaczyk

Tracks & Sign of Reptiles & Amphibians: A Guide to North American Species is another field guide I take with me when I travel.

~ Tracking Humans ~

Joel Hardin

The tracking community shares a long history. Joel Hardin was part of an early tracker group within the Border Patrol. Joel Hardin has shared some really interesting stories about that elite group of trackers, including Jack Kearney (***Tracking: A Blueprint for Learning How***, 1978) and Ab Taylor, who worked as man trackers for the Border Patrol. Currently you can find his visual human tracking school at **jhardin-inc.com**.

In 2004 he published ***Tracker: Case Files & Adventures of a Professional Mantracker*** with co-author Matt Conden. It's in my library and I read it again once in a while.

The search and rescue classes put on by Universal Tracking Services and JHPTS Visual Tracking introduced me to human tracking and trailing. The method they use to teach this is called "step by step tracking," which is an effective method for teaching people what they don't think they'll be able to see.

Fernando Moreira

I haven't taken a class from Fernando, but I would be remiss in not including him here, as I've heard many good stories about him from people who have. He's very actively teaching all over the country. Find him at **tacticaltrackingschool.com**.

David Scott Donelan

A very memorable tracker whose human tracking methods come from his time serving in the Rhodesian Army. I was invited to take one of his special classes and I'll never forget it. His school specializes in combat and tactical tracking. You can find it at **scottdonelantrackingschool.com**.

Rob Speiden

Rob is a rare animal as he is a very accomplished search-and-rescue human tracker and teacher, as well as a widely respected visual animal tracker. He has welded all the disciplines of tracking into one. He's located in Virginia. By the time you read this, he will probably have done way more than I can keep up with. If you can't catch up to him for a class or workshop, you'll find his valuable books on line. Check out the website for more information at **trackingschool.com**.

~ Bears ~

As I learned about the outdoors and being alone in the woods, bears of all kinds were fascinating to me. Probably because when I started out, they scared me to death.

When I wanted to learn more about them after a close encounter when I was out by myself, I turned to books. Most of the books about bears are bad encounters, and most of the text is devoted to the healing of bear-inflicted wounds. These books sell, though, as humans love to be scared and horrified. The titles alone promise blood and terror: *When Humans Become Prey; Mauled; A Shape in the Dark; Taken by a Bear; Fighting for Your Life; Man Eaters; Bear Attacks,* and on and on.

On the other hand, there are guides and researchers who actually spend a lot to time in the company of bears. Many Alaskans have learned to coexist very well with the bruins around them. I won't list them all here, because it is a tsunami of information, but for truthful books, based on research, try these:

Lonesome for Bears: A Woman's Journey in the Tracks of the Wilderness by Linda Jo Hunter (can't miss this one!)

In the Company of Bears: What Black Bears Have Taught Me About Intelligence and Intuition by Benjamin Kilham and Temple Grandin

Talking with Bears: Conversations with Charlie Russell by G.A. Bradshaw

Grizzly Heart: Living Without Fear Among the Brown Bears of Kamchatka by Charlie Russell and Maureen Enns

Grizzly Seasons: Life with the Brown Bears of Kamchatka by Charlie Russell and Maureen Enns

Tracking the American Black Bear by Preston Taylor

Learning to be Wild: Raising Orphan Grizzlies by Charlie Russell and Maureen Enns

In Wild Trust: Larry Aumiller's Thirty Years Among the McNeil River Brown Bears by Jeff Fair and Larry Aumiller

The Lost Grizzlies: A Search for Survivors in the Wilderness of Colorado by Rick Bass

When I was trying to find out about bears, I was shocked to discover that there lived a man who "walked with bears" in Ely, Minnesota. **Dr. Lynn Rogers** can be found online at **bearstudy.org,** the website for the Wildlife Research Institute, and at the North American Bear Center in Ely, where you, too, can visit with American black bears.

Tim Treadwell, infamous for allegedly getting himself and his girlfriend killed by bears in Alaska, is one of the most controversial bear advocates you will ever learn about. The year before he was killed, I talked with Tim on the phone for an hour or so. His experiences in living with grizzly bears shocked a lot of people and angered and provoked a lot of others.

In my conversation with him, I concluded that he wasn't crazy or stupid, but his style of in-your-face rebellion on all things everyone ever understood about bears before he came along really pushed some buttons. One of the best books I have found about him and his death is ***The Grizzly Maze: Timothy Treadwell's Fatal Obsession with Alaskan Bears*** by Nick Jans.

~ Mountain Lions (aka Cougars or Pumas) ~

Most of my knowledge about cougars, also known as mountain lions or pumas, comes from my own tracking experiences. The first came in a CyberTracker evaluation with Mark Elbroch, finding a cougar scent marking spot, a kill, some scat, and tracks. And, of course, through the book, ***Cougar Conundrum: Sharing the World with a Successful Predator*** by Mark Elbroch.

Recent research about the lives of cougars can also be accessed online at **Panthera.org,** including current projects in understanding and conservation.

~ Other Books That Have Influenced Me ~

Nick Jans, the author I mentioned above, also wrote one of my favorite books about wolves. Look for **A Wolf Called Romeo** by Nick Jans.

Although I love all of Barbara Kingsolver's books, her book **Prodigal Summer** really spoke to me.

A Dream in Polar Fog by Yuri Rytkheu and Ilona Yazhbin Chavasse is a book that, once read, can never be forgotten.

Talking with Bears: Conversations with Charlie Russell by G. A. Bradshaw

Cry of the Kalahari; Secrets of the Savana; Twenty-three Years in the African Wilderness; The Eye of the Elephant: An Epic Adventure in the African Wilderness, all by Mark and Delia Owens.

Then Delia Owens' book, ***Where the Crawdads Sing***, now a movie as well.

The Soul of an Octopus: A Surprising Exploration into the Wonder of Consciousness by Sy Montgomery

Wolfer by Carter Niemeyer and Jenny Niemeyer

Walking Home: A Traveler in the Alaskan Wilderness, a Journey into the Human Heart by Lynn Schooler. Also, ***The Blue Bear: A True Story of Friendship and Discovery in the Alaskan Wild*** by Lynn Schooler.

Lily Pond: Four Years with a Family of Beavers; God's Dog:A Celebration of the North American Coyote, and anything else you can find by Hope Ryden.

Grizzly Years: In Search of the American Wilderness by Doug Peacock

Point Last Seen by Hannah Nyala

Track of the Cat (Anna Pigeon Mysteries Book) by Nevada Barr

Indy Quillen has written a fiction series that involves tracking, survival, mystery, and adventure. Her ***Fox Walker Series*** now includes five excellent and entertaining books.

David Barbur is another fiction author who writes a fun and informative mystery series involving tracking, nature, and a bit of the supernatural just for spice. Look up his ***Tye Caine Wilderness Mystery*** series.

~ Online Resources & Apps ~

There are the avenues that we all have for finding information online, such as Google and Wikipedia, or one of the new generative AI resources such as ChatGPT or Bing (which are not always accurate). But you'll also find less common resources that are very important.

iNaturalist is a huge database on all things natural history. Look them up at **inaturalist.org** and sign up. Not only can you find out an immense amount of information, you can contribute.

Jonah Evans maintains a wonderfully educational website at **naturetracking.com**. He also offers an ***Animal Tracks*** app for your phone or tablet that you can use to replace a few of your heavy field guides. Look for ***iTrack Wildlife Pro***.

I've tried a number of apps on my iPad, which I also use for field notes and camera. The best one I have found for plant identification is ***PictureThis—Plant Identifier***. Another app I really like is ***onXbackcountry*** for navigation and trail planning.

Acknowledgments

In the thirty odd years I have been following my own path to learning all I can about our world, I have met, tracked with and learned a lot from others on similar paths.

Terry Kem and I traded tracking knowledge for several years. He showed me the small things and details of track morphology that are not part of forest tracking. Susan James is not only a fun person to take to the woods with, her natural history knowledge is extensive and she shares well. Kimber Nelson is a joy to be with in the field and notices just about everything. Jim Bruchac taught me about storytelling and Del Morris and Tina Smith were a huge help with ISPT conferences and administration. Dan Daley was with me on one of the biggest tracking finds I have ever had; he also recommended me to the Metro Camp fire program. Several CyberTracker Evaluation leaders have substantially added to my tracking knowledge; Casey McFarland, Marcus Reynerson, Phil Johnson, Brian McConnell and David Moskowittz.

Kathy Reginato was my partner in learning the secrets of the Baja desert and Drew Hamilton taught me, his boss at the time, how to be a better guide. Steve Engel introduced me to birding and how it relates to tracking.

My years working on yachts and small cruise ships I learned from scientists, wildlife artists, marine biologists, professional guides, and captains of all kinds of vessels. Kirsten and Carl Dixon, who hired Mike and I to manage one of the Within

The Wild Adventure lodges, opened the doors to outdoor experiences in Alaska I never would have been able to experience on my own.

My parents, Earl and Norma Stevens, raised us kids on a farm and let us run loose. My little brother, Bill Stevens, was my constant adventure partner for a lot of my young years. The horse I owned in my teenage years taught me how to be around big powerful animals.

And, of course, any of you who have written a book knows that it takes the efforts of others to actually publish it. I thank Lianne and Joseph Downey for all your encouragement and hard work. Mike McHugh not only encourages me to do everything I want and need to do in life, he also feeds me and takes care of half the housework and camp chores. Jane Doudney not only is my main tracking friend, she helped me come back from major surgery by taking me in the woods three times a week, even when I could only manage a lawn chair. Fortunately, I'm back on my bike and trailing animals through the bush on foot.

The Douglas squirrels, ravens, owls, and juncos who seem to be with me in the forest as constant companions have shaped my understanding of how little I actually know and I thank them profusely for existing.

And, lastly, and also most importantly, I want to thank all the bears I have met. If you want to know about being alive in this world, just listen to the bears. They were all special.

About the Author

Linda Jo Hunter is renowned in the animal tracking community for her unique tracking and trailing methods, her teaching skills, and as the author of ***Lonesome for Bears: A Woman's Journey in the Tracks of the Wilderness***. She co-founded the International Society of Professional Trackers (ISPT), and has studied with human tracking schools, an international tracking certification group, and biologists in both Alaska and Yellowstone National Park. She has worked as a brown-bear viewing guide in Alaska, and as a private yacht captain on the West Coast, one of the first women to obtain a 100-ton Master ocean operator's license. Thirty years of first-hand observation, her experience in search and rescue, and many solo adventures have enhanced her knowledge of natural history and her skills in the wild. Find her at **LindaJoHunter.com**.

Tracking Notes

Tracking Notes

Printed in the USA
CPSIA information can be obtained
at www.ICGtesting.com
CBHW021544090624
9719CB00001B/13